HEARING

HIS

VOICE

MEETING JESUS
IN THE GARDEN OF PROMISE

A DEVOTIONAL JOURNEY OF
ENCOURAGEMENT

MEREDITH SWIFT

Edited by Hope Elaine Roughton
Cover Design by germancreative @ Fiverr
Formatted by Jen Henderson @ Wild Words Formatting

TABLE OF CONTENTS

Thank you very much for reading my book!

As a token of my appreciation, please download your FREE resource "31 Days of Inspiration and Encouragement"at www.meredithswiftauthor.com

INTRODUCTION

I have not always had a personal relationship with my Lord Jesus Christ. As a young child, I can remember lying on my back on the lawn of my childhood home, gazing up at the sky, wondering whether God was up there somewhere. If I saw rays of light coming from the clouds I wondered whether I could walk right up there to God? Or could He come down to me? Who *was* He anyhow? And was He everywhere all at once? These were just a few of the questions I pondered.

As I grew older, however, the questions grew less and less. I knew *about* God but I certainly did not believe I could *know* Him; I viewed Him as a distant figure sitting up there in Heaven. I stopped wondering about who He was. I wondered even less about Jesus and I believed Christianity to be a narrow, stifling and boring religion. It was not something that I believed could satisfy my yearning to find the meaning for my life. Instead, I embarked on a quest of spirituality which led me to becoming immersed in New Age philosophy.

I was satisfied—up to a point—with my New Age beliefs. Yet still there was part of me that was absolutely raw and aching—a wound of utter loneliness that was too painful to be touched and impossible to heal. It lived within the deepest part of me and so I was therefore able to ignore it most of the time.

Yet it was there—a constant, insistent pain and a sense of lack that could never be filled nor appeased by accumulating things or experiences, nor by the generalised "love and light" of my New Age beliefs. The Universe was <u>not</u> taking care of me and I often felt like I was drowning in self-doubt and the desire to be accepted. When I met Jesus, I didn't grasp onto Him so I could save myself. Instead, I

1

accepted Him into my heart and *He* saved *me*. It was on that day I began a journey of healing and discovery, with a Savior who lovingly walked beside me, guiding me into His plan for my life.

It became natural for me to connect with Jesus daily in prayer and to seek His guidance for whatever was happening in my life. He was—and is—available to me 24/7. This book grew out of a season of my life where I was exhausted, isolated and alone. I had stepped out of a time of intense "busyness," having just gone through a divorce, resignation from my teaching job, and relocation to a larger city to access better services for my autistic daughter, who for three months had also become very unwell. I was learning that it was non-negotiable that I allowed myself the time and space needed to rest and recuperate from this very difficult and challenging time.

As part of this process, as suggested by a wonderful Christian counsellor, I began to intentionally and regularly seek out and connect with Lord Jesus, many times a day—7 times a day for 21 days, to be exact. With one of my favorite Scriptures (Psalm 46:10) as a foundation and protection, I was able to "see" Jesus, hear His voice and speak with Him in a most beautiful garden I came to know as the Garden of Promise. This garden was so lush and incredibly beautiful that I imagined it to be what the Garden of Eden must have been like, so long ago. With Scripture as my foundation and with the covering of prayer, so long as I trusted that I was meeting with Lord Jesus and that He was speaking with me, the words flowed quickly and easily. He spoke to me about many different situations and challenges of my life. As I drew close to Him, He drew close to me.

Interspersed with these conversations were my reflections about my relationship with Him. This grew into a pattern of six conversations and one reflection—rather like working six days of the week with the seventh a day of rest. Biblically, a series of 7 is identified with something being finished or complete—for example, God's creation of the world in 7 days in the Book of Genesis—so this is how the book is structured.

The process of meeting with Jesus and the subsequent recording of our conversations—which grew into this book—was life changing for me. Through the process of regular connection with Lord Jesus I was able to lose the sense of intense aloneness that had defined me. I began to feel rejuvenated by His presence and uplifted by His grace, and my personal relationship with Him deepened and broadened. His instruction and guidance as to how I could best come into His presence reinforced to me just how available He is to me, how He yearns to be in relationship with me, and how He is never too busy to spend time with me.

Dear reader—it is my hope that you are encouraged, enriched, blessed and guided by these words and Scriptures and that through them you too will draw closer to Jesus and He to you. He yearns to have a relationship with you! It is my hope that, like me, you are soothed, encouraged, inspired and uplifted by hearing His voice and His words.

I offer them to you in the mighty and transforming name of Jesus.

> *Joel 2:28*
> *"And afterward, I will pour out my Spirit on all people. Your sons and daughters will prophesy, your old men will dream dreams, your young men will see visions. Even on my servants, both men and women, I will pour out my Spirit in those days."*

> *John 14:6*
> *Jesus answered, "I am the way and the truth and the life. No one comes to the Father except through me."*

PREFACE

MEETING JESUS
IN THE GARDEN

Psalm 46:10
He said "Be still and know that I am God".

I am repeating this Scripture and imagining myself in a most lush and incredibly beautiful garden. I imagine it to be like the Garden of Eden had been. The air is fragrant with the scent of all my favorite flowers—jasmine, frangipani, roses and violets—a riot of dazzling colors. The emerald grass under my bare feet is lush and thick. Towering trees and creeping vines form a canopy of shade over me. I see a river, sparkling, and the richest, deepest shade of turquoise blue. The breeze is soft and gentle on my face and I am bathed in the warmth of a golden sun. This garden is perfect in my imagination; the perfect setting for me to meet with Jesus.

He is waiting for me. He wants me to walk with Him.

"Take my arm and we will walk together. Isn't this beautiful?" He says, gesturing with His hand. "I made this just for you My child. Isn't it wondrous? Such beauty in the world!"

I look towards the edge of the garden. There is a brick wall covered in vines. The brick wall represents the boundary between my old life and my new one.

I am able to rest in this garden. Sweet peace. I lie on that soft lush grass with my head in Jesus's lap. I feel so fully supported, so safe and secure. "Rest here with Me and let me reprogram your thoughts My darling, precious child". Jesus looks into my eyes deeply and then passes His hand over them so they gently close. His hands are on either side of my head and His voice, though low, fills my head with His resonance and opens out so that the sound comprises everything in the garden. Everything is made from His voice and His words are going to speak new life into me.

This is my Garden of Promise.

SECTION 1

ENTERING THE GARDEN

"Do not worry about anything. Cast all your cares on Me. The worry is not for you to bear but for Me to take from you. Its master is under My dominion. Trust Me that he cannot touch you—nor can his desire for you to worry. Unless you allow this.

"Rest here with Me and fix your attention on Me, My darling, precious child. This is who you are to Me. You are My precious child. This is how I see you: You are beautiful. You are precious. You are more than worthy. You are more than enough. You are completely wonderful to me. These are My promises to you: I will take care of you. I will always be with you. I love you. You can rest in Me.

"Let Me help you, precious child. Be with Me. Trust Me. I have a plan for your life that is wondrous. Only you being you will complete the part of the plan I created you for. Your part is intertwined with the parts of all My other children. It is a wondrous plan that I have for you all. Look to Me as the architect of that plan and rely on Me for guidance. Trust in Me."

> *Psalm 55:22*
> *Cast your cares on the LORD and he will sustain you;*
> *he will never let the righteous be shaken.*

> *Proverbs 3:5*
> *Trust in the LORD with all your heart*
> *and lean not on your own understanding;*
> *6 in all your ways submit to him,*
> *and he will make your paths straight.*

FIX YOUR EYES ON JESUS

"Do not be discouraged by what the outside world displays to you. Your circumstances do not define who you are. When you keep your eyes on Me, the author of your faith, you will find this easier to follow. When you fix your eyes on your eternal reward with Me, your circumstances pale by comparison. They do not matter. Only Me and your walk with Me.

"I performed many miracles during My time on earth. The biggest miracle of all is what I can do within a human heart that is softened towards Me. I walk with everyone, every minute of their existence. Sometimes they do not have eyes to see this and their hearts are hardened against Me. But that does not make this miracle any less true."

> *1 Peter 2:9*
> *But you are a chosen people, a royal priesthood, a holy nation, God's special possession, that you may declare the praises of him who called you out of darkness into his wonderful light.*

AN INTRICATE DESIGN

"What would the world look like to me if my life had been different and if I had known You earlier? Who would I be?" I ask Jesus.

"You would not be you, the you I created. The you I created to fit My plan. I exist outside of time and I see the beginning and the end of all that I created and all that is in between. I knew you at the beginning, before I spoke the world into being. Everything that has happened to you in your life is because of who I called you to be. What the enemy originally intended for evil I have turned for good. All the pain and isolation and aloneness you felt was required so that your character could be built and so that you could be equipped for the reason you are here. For you living your true purpose is a glorification of Me and My Father.

"It is intricate, My design of you. Your pain and suffering was a strong outer layer of your soul, but My Holy Spirit was stronger and came into you as I knew it would. Each lie the enemy told you held the kernel of My truth within it, like a mirror image. I knew My promises would be strong enough to draw you to Me. I knew the pain you felt could be soothed and I knew all your tears could be washed away. I knew you would choose Me just as I chose you. It could not be any other way. You live within Me now."

Psalm 139:16
Your eyes saw my unformed body,
all the days ordained for me
were written in your book
before one of them came to be.

MEREDITH SWIFT

Jeremiah 29:11
"For I know the plans I have for you," declares the LORD, "plans to
prosper you and not to harm you,
plans to give you hope and a future."

NEW THOUGHT PATTERNS

"Use your Bible to determine the focus of your new thoughts. Scripture is God breathing life into words and there is an answer for every single life situation you will ever encounter. All we need to do is tend our new thought patterns every day. Water them by reading and remembering Scripture. Think about My promises and the words I breathed into you when we first met in this garden. We are planting and creating the most beautiful garden here, a place of serenity where everything can bloom. You will bloom too. As this garden grows, so too will your new thought patterns. It's good, honest toil, building your new and replenished thought life.

"Daily toil is essential. Get your hands dirty as you undertake this honest toil, knowing I have washed you clean with My blood and your new thoughts are creations from Me to live within you.

"The influences I want are My Scriptures, a solid prayer life, communion with the Holy Spirit, and being with other believers. This is your new foundation. When you are in the world do not become too attached to what you see and experience. For you are a new creation in Me, attached to and experiencing life through Me now. Take those memories of your old life as they emerge straight to My Holy Cross and let them be washed clean, transformed with My precious blood that I shed to save you, My special, most beautiful and cherished child."

> *2 Corinthians 5:17*
> *Therefore, if anyone is in Christ, the new creation has come:*
> *The old has gone, the new is here! 18 All this is from God,*
> *who reconciled us to himself through Christ and gave us*
> *the ministry of reconciliation.*

Romans 12:2
Do not conform to the pattern of this world, but be transformed by the renewing of your mind. Then you will be able to test and approve what God's will is—his good, pleasing and perfect will.

BLOOMING IN THE GARDEN

"I am the new life, the backdrop and the foundation to your new growth. You are a flower about to bloom. Your perfume is beautiful and your petals are divine. You will grow straight and direct as you grow towards Me.

"Times of quiet are vital to our journey of growth together. Take the time to listen for My voice. You know My presence is just a heartbeat away, yet My voice, which spoke into being all of creation, can be very still and small. You will need ears to hear—you will need to stop and rest and wait on My voice.

"It is time for old cement foundations to be jackhammered and broken up into dust and ash. Replace that old cement foundation with the living solid rock of My being. I am reshaping you into who you already are. My child. So just be with Me. Let your mind imagine the new possibilities that await you in Me."

> *1 Kings 19:12*
> *After the earthquake came a fire,*
> *but the LORD was not in the fire.*
> *And after the fire came a gentle whisper.*

TRANSFORMING THE HEART

"I dwell within your heart, precious child. I look *at* your heart and *from* your heart also. There is nothing about your human heart that I do not know. Most of all, I know how to transform you from inside your heart out.

"Look to the virtues of the heart, the fruit of the spirit—kindness, patience, gentleness, love. Meditate on Me being alive! Meditate on My forgiveness! And let your heart be overflowing with the joy—profound yet simple joy—of Me saving you because of My love for you. *I love you.* I love you more deeply than you will ever, or can ever, be loved by another human. My divinity means My love is a transcending love. It is all of the beauty of the sunrise and sunset, the promise of new beginnings, and the renewal of spirit. It is a transforming love. I take you and work on and with your precious heart.

"The journey we are on is one of joy, My precious child. Those old ways were devoid of life and joy. The new ways are brimming with life and joy. Walking and talking with Me, building relationship with Me, brings an outpouring and overflowing of joy. I want you to know this, I want you to breathe this in and exhale it out. Let it start to indwell you, ask for it to permeate your dreams and guide your direction during your waking moments."

> *1 Samuel 16:7*
> *But the LORD said to Samuel, "Do not consider his appearance or his height, for I have rejected him. The LORD does not look at the things people look at. People look at the outward appearance, but the LORD looks at the heart.*

REFLECTION:
CHOOSING JESUS

"Knock and the door shall be opened unto you."

We can choose to walk through the door to Him. We are not forced to do this. The choice can be camouflaged with fear or doubt. This is because the enemy does not want us to choose Jesus. One of the most incredible things about knowing Jesus is knowing that He has given us all free will. He could easily force us to have a relationship with Him. But he does not force. Just as he freely gave His life on the Cross, so too must we freely give our lives to Him.

He never asks us to do what He Himself has not been prepared to do. He experienced all of life's challenges when He walked the earth as a man. God come to earth as man. He has known the challenges of race, culture, poverty, condemnation, judgement, isolation, loneliness, and so much more. He has been where you and I are, and He meets us at our deepest need and brings His healing grace as a soothing balm for our deepest pain. His is the healing that transforms. He changes our hearts so that we can be free to truly love one another the way He loves—unconditionally.

And oh, how His heart breaks at the thought of even one of His flock being lost by not turning to Him. He wants us all to turn to Him, to be with Him in relationship and for all Eternity. So choose Him. Choose Jesus and let Him come into your heart.

Matthew 7:7
Ask, and it will be given to you,
seek, and you will find,
knock and the door will be opened to you.

1 Corinthians 10:13
No temptation has overtaken you except what is common to mankind.
And God is faithful; he will not let you be tempted beyond what you can
bear. But when you are tempted, he will also provide a way out so that you
can endure it.

SECTION 2

"AM I NOT BIGGER
THAN ALL OF THIS?"

"Each day is a renewal, and each moment of each day can be a renewal too. New life through right choosing is a heartbeat away. The free will that I gave to you can be your slave or your master. I have come to set the captives free.

"You are not enslaved to your old thoughts any longer. Lay them all out in a row by writing them down and shine My light of truth on them. My promises for you are all throughout Scripture. Some days you will have to cling to these promises and to My hem. That is why I am here. Other days will be easier. Yet still cling on to Me.

"The enemy of this world wants you to cling to your worries. But that is not the way. You know I am the way. So trust in Me, cling to Me, and I will renew your mind, I will renew all about you. I renewed your heart the day you gave your life to Me, and I continue each moment to do this, until the day I call you Home. Our journey is one of togetherness now. You will never walk alone again.

"You are royalty, My precious child. I am your King and you are part of My kingdom. Go boldly into the world as befits royalty. Stand tall."

Psalm 118:24
The LORD has done it this very day;
let us rejoice today and be glad.

Jeremiah 29:12
"Then you will call on me and come and pray to me,
and I will listen to you. 13 You will seek me and find me when you seek

me with all your heart. 14 I will be found by you," declares the LORD, "and will bring you back from captivity."

A STORMY OCEAN

"Keep your eyes on Me. Imagine you are with all the other disciples in the boat with Peter. You see Me walking on the water. Could you walk to Me? If you keep your eyes on Me you will forget that there is a storm raging around you; you won't dwell on the water beneath your feet and the idea that you can't walk on water. Only if you keep your eyes on Me."

"Stay awake for Me. Keep your eyes open for the opportunity to see Me in everyone you meet and to reach out in My Holy name. When you rest, do so in Me. I am the Way, the Truth, and the Life. I am the Word made flesh. My Word is still holding this world and the universes together. My Word is still speaking truth into the hearts of non-believers so that they may be convicted and turn to Me. Just as I am the Word made flesh, so too are you My Word made flesh. You are part of the body of Christ, the hands and feet. I knit you together in your mother's womb and you are alive now in Me. Like the safe waters of your mother's womb, you are cushioned and softened within Me. I am the water; the living water that surrounds you now, just like that of your mother's womb.

"When you are parched and thirsty and the circumstances of life are drier than a desert, look upwards towards Me and ask for My living water to flow through your veins. I renew your strength and give you My strength. I stand behind you, My arms wrapped around you, to protect you from the influences of the evil one. Keep your eyes on your eternal reward, which is to be with Me in Paradise forever. That must be your motivation. I want to say, 'Well done, good and faithful servant,' when we finally meet in person on that glorious day."

Matthew 14:25-33

Shortly before dawn Jesus went out to them, walking on the lake. 26 When the disciples saw him walking on the lake, they were terrified. "It's a ghost," they said, and cried out in fear. 27 But Jesus immediately said to them: "Take courage! It is I. Don't be afraid." 28 "Lord, if it's you," Peter replied, "tell me to come to you on the water." 29. "Come," he said. Then Peter got down out of the boat, walked on the water and came toward Jesus. 30 But when he saw the wind, he was afraid and, beginning to sink, cried out, "Lord, save me! 31 Immediately Jesus reached out his hand and caught him, "You of little faith," he said, "why did you doubt?"32 And when they climbed into the boat, the wind died down. 33 Then those who were in the boat worshiped him, saying, "Truly you are the Son of God."

Matthew 25:21

His master replied, 'Well done, good and faithful servant! You have been faithful with a few things; I will put you in charge of many things. Come and share your master's happiness!'

COME TO JESUS

"A pebble is smooth and sweet in your hand, but place it in your shoe and it niggles and creates discomfort. The pebble represents the potential of a problem—if left hidden and allowed to stay inside your shoe it can become a burden. When brought out to the light and examined it can be seen for what it is—just a pebble.

"Yet it could have been anything inside that shoe. So it is with your belief systems, My child. They could be anything.

"Bring them out to the light, examine them, and then give them to Me. Let them be transformed according to My promises. I celebrate you; I honor you as My child. You are worthy and I love you more than you will ever know.

"Just keep your eyes on Me. I will never forsake you."

> *Joshua 1:5*
> *No one will be able to stand against you all the days of your life. As I was with Moses, so I will be with you; I will never leave you nor forsake you.*

SUCH A SAVIOR!

"The sun going down is like a phase of your life that is ending. After a time of rest and renewal the sun will rise again, and the sky will be lit up with such a wondrous display of color and beauty. It heralds a new beginning.

"But first you must sleep and replenish in order to be ready to greet this new day. While you walk this earth it is as though you are asleep to the true majesty of the new day that awaits you in Paradise, where you will dwell with Me forever. Eagerly fix your eyes on this day, My dearest child. It is My promise to you—and I always keep My promises.

"You are Mine and I am yours. Remember this always."

> *Luke 1:78-79*
> *because of the tender mercy of our God, by which the rising sun will come to us from heaven 79 to shine on those living in darkness and in the shadow of death, to guide our feet into the path of peace.*

> *Romans 14:8*
> *If we live, we live for the Lord; and if we die, we die for the Lord. So, whether we live or die, we belong to the Lord.*

THE JOY OF THE PRESENT

"Pure joy! If you seek Me you will know pure joy! I have created this world for you, for My glory. You are My jewel in the crown.

"I want you to be in the moment now. Do not worry about the past, for it is gone. The future is with Me; you do not need to fuss over it. Veering between the two causes you to forsake the present. The enemy wants to keep you in a state of inertia, in that no-man's-land where you are dwelling on the past and fearing for the future.

"Come into the present and fill it now with thoughts of Me, with My Scriptures, with My praise and worship, with prayer and supplication to the God of Ages who dwells in you through the provision of the Holy Spirit.

"The father of lies seeks to devour your time by indecision and frozenness, but I am here to assure you that when your eyes are on Me, in the present, this cannot happen. The enemy is defeated.

"So start realizing that your time on Earth is precious. You will never walk this way again! Glorify Me, keep your eyes on Me every moment, as then the enemy cannot drag you down into taking your precious time away. You may not realize how important you are and that there is not a moment to waste.

"Yet I am your God of timing, all comes to you in accordance with My perfect time. The time is *now* and the person is *you*! So step forward boldly into what I have for you and into your true purpose and identity. You are loved so deeply and this love is your sustenance and your substance. Trust in Me."

Psalm 16:11
You make known to me the path of life;
you will fill me with joy in your presence,
with eternal pleasures at your right hand.

Isaiah 40:31
but those who hope in the LORD
will renew their strength.
They will soar on wings like eagles;
they will run and not grow weary,
they will walk and not be faint.

DAILY LIFE CHALLENGES

"I created all this—the animals, the sun, the sky, the flowers, the trees, the vine. And YOU! The majesty of My creation is something for you to consider when you think I cannot be of help to you in your thousand different challenges of daily life. I am your Creator, the Creator of all that is.

"Your worries are not yet created; they exist yet they have no substance to them. This is because they are the domain of the enemy—the worry, anxiety, helplessness, and powerlessness is his delight and his specialty. But they are not real—unlike what I have created. The enemy wants you to *believe* they are real, and every time you do, the chains of your bondage grip a little tighter. Believe in Me. Believe in My promises. Draw near to Me by handing over your worries straightaway. I will snatch you from the enemy's hand by taking your worries away.

"Be of good cheer because I have overcome the world. When you are heavy and laden by what appears to be real in this world, lighten that burden by giving it straight to Me. I rejoice when you do this. Your persecuted brothers and sisters who are suffering unspeakable torment in My name rejoice in these sufferings because they know I am the overcomer. They keep their eyes on the prize.

"Your worries are not real. Do not allow the enemy to fool you. I care more for you than anything else in creation and I will take care of all your needs. Rest and trust in Me."

Genesis 50:20
You intended to harm me, but God intended it for good to accomplish what is now being done, the saving of many lives.

John 16:33

"I have told you these things, so that in me you may have peace. In this world you will have trouble. But take heart! I have overcome the world."

REFLECTION:
SETTING THE CAPTIVES FREE

He is hanging on the Cross and I am at His feet. I am looking up at Him and I am so anguished I can barely breathe. There are no words to describe how I am feeling. I feel responsible because of my fallen nature, from the choice made by Adam and Eve and carried through them to all mankind—to break the perfect relationship between them and God Almighty. If I had not sinned, Jesus would not have had to die to take away my sin and the sin of the world.

Yet this was the only way. It is one part of the redemptive process. Jesus was fully willing to die for me. There was no other way for the debt to be paid, for the sin to be transformed, and for the captives to be set free. Jesus came to teach, to heal, to love, and to ultimately save; a saving grace that is available to all of us. I cannot just think of and be totally anguished and humbled by His sacrifice; I must also think of Him rising and overcoming death.

Death lost its sting 2000 years ago and now, today, my Savior Jesus Christ, Lord of all creation, is real and clear and close and present with me in a relationship that is personal and transforming. I die to self to follow Him. I fix my eyes on my risen Lord, the Lord Jesus Christ. And I thank You Jesus, for this, I thank You—every second, I thank You.

Luke 24:2
They found the stone rolled away from the tomb, 3 but when they entered, they did not find the body of the Lord Jesus.

John 17:1
After Jesus said this, he looked toward heaven and prayed: "Father, the

hour has come. Glorify your Son, that your Son may glorify you. 2 For you granted him authority over all people that he might give eternal life to all those you have given him. 3 Now this is eternal life: that they know you, the only true God, and Jesus Christ, whom you have sent. 4 I have brought you glory on earth by finishing the work you gave me to do. 5 And now, Father, glorify me in your presence with the glory I had with you before the world began."

SECTION 3

YOUR WORDS ARE
LIKE ARROWS

"You are a warrior with your breastplate of righteousness and your shield of truth. Your thoughts are like the arrows which go forth. Make sure they are thoughts and arrows of the abundance that is found in Me, the riches that dwell in Me as your Creator and Savior.

"Your words are also like arrows. Once they are shot forth they can go a long way and cannot be retracted. Some will hurt, others will wound. If your intent is to edify and build up others with your words the arrow will pierce their heart and open it a little more. If not, the arrow will pierce their heart and wound. Words are precious and powerful. They connect everything together.

"I spoke the world into being with My Word; I am the Word became flesh and dwelling in man. Decide to use only words of power, beauty, and truth. But first guard that your thoughts do not become words of destruction and that your arrows do not wound or kill. Only then will you know how to be a true warrior. Self-control is essential. Mindfulness. The battle begins in the mind. It can end in the mind also.

"Take your thoughts to the Cross—My Holy Cross—and ask that these thoughts be transformed by the power of My Holy and precious blood spilled out for you and washing you clean. All is done; you need do no more. Only rest in Me and I can guide you. I can steer your rudderless ship safely into the harbor of My love and My Father's glorification.

Go hard at this task, for you have countless thoughts that occupy your mind every day. Empty out those thoughts that are not of Me and the enemy will weaken and be defeated even more. Be strong and courageous, for I have given you a spirit not of fear but of boldness.

You are My warrior, dear child, in the spiritual battle raging all around you.

"The enemy's time runs short so he pulls out all the stops. We want people off that fence and into the Kingdom. One path leads to destruction, the other to glorification and victory in Jesus Christ your Savior—the Savior and Creator of this world and all the worlds beyond. Do not fear but rather rejoice in the love of your Father, which sets you free from the bondage of the limitations your enemy wants you to think are real. They are not. Only focus on Me, the Way, the Truth, and the Life forever and forever. For Mine is the kingdom, the power and glory forever and ever. Amen."

> *Ephesians 6:14*
> *Stand firm then, with the belt of truth buckled around your waist, with the breastplate of righteousness in place, 15 and with your feet fitted with the readiness that comes from the gospel of peace. 16 In addition to all this, take up the shield of faith, with which you can extinguish all the flaming arrows of the evil one. 17 Take the helmet of salvation and the sword of the Spirit, which is the word of God.*

MUCH MORE THAN SURVIVAL

"Be like a little child and trust without needing answers or reasons as to why something happened a certain way. Know this: that the past is gone forever. Keep on dying to yourself and being renewed in Me. When My Holy Spirit enters into you as a believer it burns away all the dross that is not needed. It remakes you minute by minute, second by second, into one who is more like Me. And this pleases Me.

"And like a little child who does not question its parents' ability to provide, trust in Me to provide for your every need. Right here and right now, are you not breathing in and out? Are you not fed? Are you not clothed? Are you not sheltered? I have the ability to pour out a blessing, to fill you to overflowing. Only trust. My plans are for you to prosper. The enemy's plans are for you to lack. The thoughts of this world are overwhelmingly of lack because the enemy delights in this. It keeps people in bondage and in survival. I promise more, much more for you than mere survival.

"I promise blessing upon blessing. And the greatest blessing I have given is to finish the work of sin and bring forgiveness to the captives so that they may be set free. You only need to give to Me, rest in Me, trust in Me. I will never leave you nor forsake you. You are now under grace, which in and of itself is a fathomless, limitless ocean of serenity and letting go. Let go of your old life and hold onto Me."

Malachi 3:10
Bring the whole tithe into the storehouse, that there may be food in my house. Test me in this," says the LORD Almighty, "and see if I will not throw open the floodgates of heaven and pour out so much blessing that there will not be room enough to store it."

Matthew 11:28

"Come to me, all you who are weary and burdened, and I will give you rest. 29 Take my yoke upon you and learn from me, for I am gentle and humble in heart, and you will find rest for your souls. 30 For my yoke is easy and my burden is light."

A PERSONAL RELATIONSHIP

"You are always My child and you never have to leave My safety and security. I am the calm amongst the raging waves; I am the light shining from the clay jar; I am your Savior hanging on a Cross because I wanted to give My life for you! I wanted to give you an eternal relationship with Me, one where you live under grace and have the opportunity for healing forgiveness to transform your life. I have been in every life situation that ever existed. You are no longer condemned under Adam's Law but instead sanctified under grace.

"Each of My children is able to have this personal one-on-one relationship with Me. That is what I desire and hope for more than anything, that fellowship between Myself and My children. Come into My throne room and be with Me, My precious child, My beautiful one. Let Me redeem you.

"No matter where you have been I have been there with you, I am present where you are going, and I arrive before you—every time. One thing only—keep your eyes on Me. I love you."

> *Psalm 139:7*
> *Where can I go from your Spirit?*
> *Where can I flee from your presence?*
> *8 If I go up to the heavens, you are there;*
> *if I make my bed in the depths, you are there.*
> *9 If I rise on the wings of the dawn,*
> *if I settle on the far side of the sea,*
> *10 even there your hand will guide me,*
> *your right hand will hold me fast.*

Luke 8:16

*"No one lights a lamp and hides it in a clay jar or puts it under a bed.
Instead, they put it on a stand, so that those who come in can see the light."*

BEING INTENTIONAL

"Be intentional.

"Intentionally welcome the Holy Spirit into your being each and every day.

"Pray for the Holy Spirit's guidance to come.

"Get quiet and prepare for the Holy Spirit to come.

"I left the Holy Spirit with you when I ascended back to My Father.

"Spend time with the Holy Spirit now. Quiet time."

> *John 16:13*
> *But when he, the Spirit of truth, comes, he will guide you into all the truth. He will not speak on his own; he will speak only what he hears, and he will tell you what is yet to come.*

> *Romans 8:9*
> *You, however, are not in the realm of the flesh but are in the realm of the Spirit, if indeed the Spirit of God lives in you. And if anyone does not have the Spirit of Christ, they do not belong to Christ.*

UNLIMITED MIND

"Your body may be limited but your mind is not. Paul did some of My mightiest work from a prison cell; beaten, tortured, and praising, praising, praising. The body is not what is important. It is the mind and the heart.

"The mind in particular is the source of limiting beliefs and it is where the battle is usually lost or won. The heart, however, transcends the mind and this is what I look at; I look at the heart. The heart is what I purify when My children give themselves to Me. And then we work on releasing the mind from the bondage and the lies of the enemy. If I am beside you it will not matter if you are in a prison cell or back in the beautiful garden you are growing accustomed to inhabiting.

"Trust in Me. Listen for My voice. The sheep know the voice of the shepherd, their protector and their deliverer."

My thoughts: Just as David fought wild and fierce beasts to protect his flock, so too does Jesus protect us against the roaring, prowling enemy who seeks to destroy. Yet Jesus rises from the dead and has transcended death Himself. It has lost its sting. The things of this world grow strangely dim as His light radiates through this lost and broken world. Thank You, Jesus!

> *1 Peter 5:8*
> *Be alert and of sober mind. Your enemy the devil prowls around like a roaring lion looking for someone to devour. 9 Resist him, standing firm in the faith, because you know that the family of believers throughout the world is undergoing the same kind of sufferings. 10 And the God of all grace, who called you to his eternal glory in Christ, after you have suffered a little*

while, will himself restore you and make you strong, firm and steadfast. 11 To him be the power for ever and ever. Amen.

PRAISE AND WORSHIP

"Praise and worship is restorative, linking us together and bringing joy with gratitude. Praise and worship at every opportunity. In times of trouble when you are casting your cares on Me, praise and worship Me because that will uplift you. You cannot praise and worship and worry at the same time. Praise and worship takes your focus and attention away from your troubles.

"It can always be done, even if you think you have no voice. The power of the voice and the words together cannot be underestimated. It does so much more than you know when you praise and worship Me. And when you praise and worship with other believers there is a purity of intention that is immeasurable. I hear it. Always. It sends out a strong signal and silences the enemy.

"I love you, My dearest child. I am always happy to spend time with you."

> *Psalm 28:6*
> *Praise be to the LORD,*
> *for he has heard my cry for mercy,*
> *7 The LORD is my strength and my shield;*
> *my heart trusts in him, and he helps me.*
> *My heart leaps for joy,*
> *and with my song I praise him.*

> *Acts 16:25*
> *About midnight Paul and Silas were praying and singing hymns to God,*
> *and the other prisoners were listening to them. 26 Suddenly there was such*

a violent earthquake that the foundations of the prison were shaken. At once all the prison doors flew open, and everyone's chains came loose.

REFLECTION:
THEN AS NOW

Things were not that different 2,000 years ago. The same challenges and the same issues people faced then are what we are facing now. Back then, as it is now, people were still rebellious, disobedient, immoral, selfish and self-seeking, worshiping hundreds if not thousands of different idols, and living without love or regard for their fellow man.

The Holy word of Jesus is as relevant today, in this hurting and lost world, as it was back in Old and New Testament times. It provides the solution to every challenge faced in life. Its authors were flawed, imperfect human beings whom God used mightily.

And that is His message today—that even though you may feel like you are insignificant in so many ways, you can be used mightily if you surrender to God and the plan He has for your life. "In your weakness, I make you strong—for if you were not weak, you would not need Me to help you and guide you. Just obey and trust. Trust and obey."

> *Philippians 4:11*
> *I am not saying this because I am in need, for I have learned to be content whatever the circumstances. 12 I know what it is to be in need, and I know what it is to have plenty. I have learned the secret of being content in any and every situation, whether well fed or hungry, whether living in plenty or in want. 13 I can do all this through him who gives me strength.*

SECTION 4

ARE YOU READY FOR
THE LORD'S RETURN?

"If I were to come to you today, would you be ready? Would your house be in order? Or would you feel let down by your own inadequacies? I do not see what you are judging within yourself as inadequacy. I see beautiful broken pieces that can be knit together and made whole within Me. That is what I see.

"Yet I urge you to live each day prayerfully and with the hopeful expectation that this day is the day that I will come back and claim My Bride again. Be the light that this hurting and lost world so desperately needs. Live each day in remembrance and anticipation of Me. Take up your Cross and follow Me. Die to yourself every day by eagerly looking towards Me and following Me. Be My disciple in that your discipline each day is to live as I have shown you.

"Love one another as I have loved you and love the Lord your God with all your heart, soul, and mind. Do not look downwards and downcast at the apparent woes of your life. But look upwards and forwards to Me. Take My outstretched hand and recognize our partnership each and every minute of the day. Live simply. Clear out your mind so it can be filled with Me.

"I see who you are. *I see who you are*. I claimed you as Mine the day you turned to Me and repented of your old sinful lifestyle. I see who you are! And I rejoice in the perfection of who I created you to be. You are My precious child who I will never forsake and who I will always encourage and direct, through My Holy Spirit and through your remembrance of Me and what I finished on the Cross.

"So look forward to the day we will meet again and let this be your yardstick by which you live each of your todays. Your yesterdays are lost and gone now—bury them—let them go as I have let your sin go and remember it no more. It is banished from My mind. Let it also be banished from yours. For I am the Kingdom, the power, and the glory, forever and ever. Amen."

Isaiah 43:25
I, even I, am he who blots out your transgressions,
for my own sake, and remembers your sins no more.

Luke 10:27
He answered, "'Love the Lord your God with all your heart
and with all your soul and with all your strength and with all your mind';
and, 'Love your neighbor as yourself.'"

LIVING WATER

"My living water is powerful. Walk in the world with an awareness that you are in a protective tunnel and this protection is through My provision. I have conquered death and all of nature and creation bows to Me.

"You are moving through a tunnel right now, bridging an old world and a new one. The old way is the beliefs you have left behind, washed clean by My Holy blood and My living water.

"You are moving through a tunnel, like a birth canal, into a new life. You cannot imagine what this new life holds for you, but you know My promises are that I have a plan for your life and I shower you with My goodness and grace. So look forward and step into the created purpose I have for you."

John 7:37
On the last and greatest day of the festival, Jesus stood and said in a loud voice, "Let anyone who is thirsty come to me and drink. 38 Whoever believes in me, as Scripture has said, rivers of living water will flow from within them."

BUSY, BUSY, BUSY

"Being constantly busy is like worshiping an idol. Even those people doing for Me can fall prey to this trap. Because I did everything for you when I died on the Cross, there is actually nothing more that needs to be done except be in relationship with Me.

"Do less, pray more, be with Me more, have more quiet time. Read My Word. Be in My presence. If you are too busy you will end up so exhausted and burnt out that you will not hear My still, small voice nor the whisperings of My Holy Spirit sent to guide you.

"Even if you believe you are doing for Me, in My name, if you are too busy-busy there really is no time for our relationship. I want our relationship to flourish, not wilt through lack of care and time together. My relationship with you requires care and attention and quality time. Be with Me more, do for Me less and have the relationship with Me that I desire from all of My children.

"What is more important than Me? Slow down. Quiet down. Remove any distractions from your life that hinder your relationship with Me. Put Me back into the center of your life. It is where I want to be."

> *Luke 10:38*
> *As Jesus and his disciples were on their way, he came to a village where a woman named Martha opened her home to him. 39 She had a sister called Mary, who sat at the Lord's feet listening to what he said. 40 But Martha was distracted by all the preparations that had to be made. She came to him and asked, "Lord, don't you care that my sister has left me to do the work by myself? Tell her to help me!" 41 "Martha, Martha," the Lord*

answered, "you are worried and upset about many things, 42 but few things are needed—or indeed only one. Mary has chosen what is better, and it will not be taken away from her."

Philippians 4:6
Do not be anxious about anything, but in every situation, by prayer and petition, with thanksgiving, present your requests to God. 7 And the peace of God, which transcends all understanding, will guard your hearts and your minds in Christ Jesus.

FALLING TEARS

"Your tears, your sorrow, and your repentance of your actions in life are all part of relinquishing the hold of the past. Through these and with your tears you can be purged of what is unnecessary to your life any longer.

"The tears soften your spirit. You lose control when you cry and the tears release, release, release you. If you are one who finds it hard to cry, give yourself permission to do so.

"Remember that in your weakness I am made strong to lift you up and carry you. The perception that tears are a weakness is distorted; the tears show you are human and they are necessary for your health.

"My promise is that I shall wipe away every tear when we unite forever in Paradise. Look forward to that glorious day when there will be no more suffering, no more tears, just joy everlasting as we reunite forever."

2 Corinthians 12:9
But he said to me, "My grace is sufficient for you, for my power is made perfect in weakness. Therefore I will boast all the more gladly about my weaknesses, so that Christ's power may rest on me."

Revelation 21:4
'He will wipe away every tear from their eyes. There will be no more death or mourning or crying or pain, for the old order of things has passed away.'

REST IN JESUS

"Rest in Me. Drop that burden and rest in Me. For My yoke is light.

"Rest is essential. Not merely physical rest but also spiritual rest. A rest from the busyness of life. A rest from the natural world. When you enter into covenant with Me and refresh your parched spirit, then that is the best rest you will ever know. Do less and accomplish more when you are able to rest in Me. I can pick up where you can leave off.

"But this involves surrender. Surrendering your will to Mine own and trusting in My guidance and the plan I have for your life. Have I not promised you? Obedience is essential. Trust and obey and I will give you rest and guidance. I am the Alpha and the Omega, the beginning and the end. Now rest, My dearest child. Rest."

Psalm 37:7
Be still before the Lord
and wait patiently for him;
do not fret when people succeed in their ways,
when they carry out their wicked schemes.

Hebrews 4:9
There remains, then, a Sabbath rest for the people of God; 10 for anyone who enters God's rest also rests from their works, just as God did from his. 11 Let us, therefore, make every effort to enter that rest, so that no one will perish by following their example of disobedience.

MY GREATEST CREATION

"Humankind is My greatest creation. The blood flowing through your veins, the breath in your lungs, your internal organs, the wondrous mechanism of your hands and feet, the amazing interlocking mastery of your eyes, ears, nose and mouth—the intricacies of your bodily system and the way everything works together. All of these are wondrous within themselves, either individually or as the sum of the whole.

"Yet more miraculous than this is how I have connected all of you with each other. Humans are bonded together whether you realize this or not; through your brains, your hearts and your minds.

"More intricate than any of this is the uniqueness of each of you. Your fingerprints are not the same as any other's. My fingerprints on you are not the same as any other's. You are fearfully and wonderfully made. Fearfully—to be amazed by! You are amazing to Me, totally amazing! There is no one like you. It goes beyond you being special. You are one of a kind.

"And within each of you I built a heart-shaped hole that can only be filled with Me. Make it your mission, with My help, to reveal the purpose I have created you for. Glorify Me through the process of finding this out.

"Ask Me for guidance and you will find it. Ask, and the door shall be opened, seek and you will find, knock and the door will be opened. I am here for you 24/7 to talk with, to be questioned, and to assist in so many, many ways. I love you and I am waiting for you to tap into the uniqueness of your created self. My one and only, most precious child. I love you totally and completely and for always.

"Have eyes that truly see, have a mouth that speaks words of encouragement and truth and sings praises to Me. Do not let your words be wasted, petty, and shallow. Listen for My voice always so you may hear when I speak to you. Abide in Me."

Genesis 1:27
So God created mankind in his own image, in the image
of God he created them; male and female he created them.

2 Corinthians 5:20
We are therefore Christ's ambassadors,
as though God were making his appeal through us.
We implore you on Christ's behalf: Be reconciled to God.

REFLECTION:
THE WEAK BECOME STRONG

The words of the Bible come alive to me. I am there journeying with the apostles, with Joseph in the pit, in the desert with Moses and in prison with Paul. I am with Samson as, blinded and shorn, he brings down the pillars on the Pharisees. And I am with Jonah in the belly of that whale. I am with each of these men and also the women of faith in the Scriptures, and their story is my story.

For that is what the Bible is—holiness in the person of ordinary men and women yoked with the perfection of an immaculate Creator to do what seems impossible to man. Over and over again, God's miraculous hand moves and mountains melt. Time and time again, the weak become strong through the power of the Lord God Almighty.

The Holy Spirit is the revelatory guide that brings these Holy Scriptures to life, which shines the light on these words and applies them practically to every imaginable situation in life. We do not have a Savior who has not experienced all that we as frail humans encounter. We have a Savior who has tasted life, who has drunk it in so completely, yet who has remained sinless and perfect so that He could become the bridge between Heaven and Earth, so that He could smash the enemy's power over death, and so that He could offer the covenant that would never again be broken.

And we are with Him on that Cross, nailed up there with Him, dead to our old lives and resurrected with Him, entering into His wound and absorbed as believers into His body, the body of Christ. Our perfect High Priest whose life was perfectly aligned with the will of His Father, and who in perfect obedience submitted to that will so that His purpose could be accomplished.

Oh that we may also glorify our Father through the submission and offering of our lives to Him!

> *Amos 9:5*
> *The Lord, the LORD Almighty—he touches the earth and it melts, and all who live in it mourn; the whole land rises like the Nile, then sinks like the river of Egypt; 6 he builds his lofty palace in the heavens and sets its foundations on the earth; he calls for the waters of the sea and pours them out over the face of the land—the LORD is his name.*

> *Ephesians 4:20*
> *That, however, is not the way of life you learned 21 when you heard about Christ and were taught in him in accordance with the truth that is in Jesus. 22 You were taught, with regard to your former way of life, to put off your old self, which is being corrupted by its deceitful desires; 23 to be made new in the attitude of your minds; 24 and to put on the new self, created to be like God in true righteousness and holiness.*

SECTION 5

"I HAVE NOT GIVEN
YOU A SPIRIT OF FEAR"

"What are you so afraid of? Your fears are that which the enemy has spoken into your being at different stages of your life, opinions formed, but which are in reality utterly formless and without foundation, impressed upon you simply because you were impressionable and then allowed to become strongholds within you. You are sensitive and this sensitivity honed in on lies that the enemy sought to make you believe.

"But I work beyond the lies spoken and the words of damage. I work on the heart and I bring your attention to My foundational promise for your life—'I have not given you a spirit of fear.' Fears are not real. Your spirit is not fearful; it is rich, powerful, brave, enthusiastic, loving, gentle, seeking, and wise. You are My child and I want you to shake those lies out of your body, shake them out of your mind and heart. They do not serve you and they have kept you in bondage long enough. Relinquish them all to Me and I will transform them at the foot of My Holy Cross. We speak words of truth into your life now in My name, in the mighty name of Jesus. And the truth is what will set you free.

"My Word spoke all into creation. The enemy's words seek to destroy what and how and who I have created. He hates you with a vengeance because you belong to Me. And you hear My voice. Turn to Me and we will silence the enemy's voice. You will know it is his voice when you feel dead within yourself.

"When it is My voice I bring Life and abundance with Me. There is expansion and the knowledge that circumstances may come and go, but I, the light of the world, am eternal. You, as My child, stand strong in your faith and walk beside Me. The enemy has been defeated. Come alive in Me, precious child, and walk forward into the truth of who you are . . . My created and loved and cherished child."

> *John 8:12*
> *When Jesus spoke again to the people, he said,*
> *"I am the light of the world. Whoever follows me*
> *will never walk in darkness, but will have the light of life."*

> *John 10:10*
> *The thief comes only to steal and kill and destroy;*
> *I have come that they may have life, and have it to the full.*

TRUST AND FAITH

"Have a trust that is absolute without all the mind intellectualizations and rationalizations and need for proof that so many times an adult perspective demands. A child is always smaller than its world. It takes this for granted; that there are always many more things bigger than itself.

"And so it needs to be this way with faith. Just accept and trust that there is a God who loves you and who created you for a wonderful life. This is the truth even if you do not believe that it is. It is an unalterable fact.

"Fix your eyes on the One who promises all, on the One who died for you and who wants to have a relationship with you. And then give yourself over to that love, that total, beautiful love that does not have its origins in world view but rather in Creator view—made in His image; good."

> *Matthew 18:2*
> *He called a little child to him, and placed the child among them. 3 And he said: "Truly I tell you, unless you change and become like little children, you will never enter the kingdom of heaven. 4 Therefore, whoever takes the lowly position of this child is the greatest in the kingdom of heaven. 5 And whoever welcomes one such child in my name welcomes me.*

> *Romans 5:1*
> *Therefore, since we have been justified through faith, we have peace with God through our Lord Jesus Christ, 2 through whom we have gained access by faith into this grace in which we now stand. And we boast in the hope of the glory of God.*

YOU MAKE A DIFFERENCE

"I hear you saying you don't make a difference, My child, but I am here to tell you that you do. You are an intricate part of a complex design, the story of mankind's fall from grace and perfect relationship with God, through to the redemptive plan and the restoration of that perfect relationship when we are together in Paradise. You were created for the glory of God and the limiting beliefs you have are just masking the perfect plan that these communications are part of.

"It is like ripples on the water caused by a tiny stone being thrown. The ripples begin small and then move outward in ever-larger circles. Each believer has a ripple effect through word and action as they walk through the world. When you live in accordance with the will of God your ripple effect becomes that much bigger, more than you realise.

"So never question how I could have saved one such as you; the simple truth is that your salvation was never an issue and never in doubt, yet was set in place at the beginning of time in this fallen world.

"Rest assured, My precious child, I have known and loved you for all Eternity and this will never change. I love you."

> *Zephaniah 3:17*
> *The LORD your God is with you, the Mighty Warrior who saves. He will take great delight in you; in his love he will no longer rebuke you, but will rejoice over you with singing.*

> *Romans 8:37*
> *No, in all these things we are more than conquerers through him who loved us.*

LEAN INTO JESUS

"Lay down with Me as in lush green pasture, rest in Me, rest in My Word, rest in My love, rest in the promises I have made that I will always keep. Cease your orchestrations and your need to control all that is around you. It is impossible to hang on all the time. You grow weary fast, and the weariness becomes exhaustion, and the exhaustion becomes burn-out. I ask you to rest in Me.

"This means lean into Me, drink in My Word, pray unceasingly, look to Me as the solution to all that plagues you. Because I Am. Rest in Me. Look at Me, *really* look at Me, keep your eyes on Me, hold fast to Me. Your focus on Me will allay the restlessness and the distraction that the enemy specializes in. When you are restless and distracted it is far easier for the enemy to gain a foothold.

"Rest. Rest. Rest in Me. And I will quench your thirst and fill you with My living water to soothe you and replenish you. Let go, My child, of what you think you should be doing. I have done all there is to do. Get quiet and still and rest. Know that I am with you and I yearn for relationship with you and for us to spend time together.

"Rest in Me. I will grant you the peace that surpasses all understanding. Rest in Me. Now."

> *1 Kings 5:4*
> *But now the LORD my God has given me rest*
> *on every side; and there is no adversary or disaster.*

John 15:5

I am the vine, you are the branches. If you remain in me and I in you, you will bear much fruit; apart from me you can do nothing.

YOU ARE ROYALTY

"You are royalty—part of a royal priesthood, child of a King, subject of a Kingdom.

"Remember that you are royalty when you are tempted to discount your worth or tempted to believe you do not matter. You were raised into royalty when you invited Me into your heart. Your life can never be the same again, for I have raised you into royalty. And My Kingdom is yours also. You are to further the advancement of the Kingdom by preaching My gospel. This is the Great Commission.

"You are to go about your daily life with the knowledge that you are the child of a King, and carry out your daily tasks with this in mind. I am your King and you are raised into royalty. Beautiful. Worthy. Uniquely created.

"I became sin so that you could be made righteous and inherit My Kingdom, Paradise eternal. My grace flowed in equal measures with My blood as I took on past, present, and future sin so that I could be in moment to moment relationship with you, My most beautiful and cherished child.

"Repent daily and renew your mind daily, as these actions will bring you closer to Me."

My thoughts: The deepest and purest love and utter tenderness has me falling to my knees and then I lay at His feet, the feet of my King. In all of the moments of my life there is no moment more precious to me than the realization that my King loves me and wants to be with me. My perfect Savior. My Lord Jesus Christ.

Isaiah 62:3
You will be a crown of splendor in the LORD's hand,
a royal diadem in the hand of your God.

Matthew 28:16
Then the eleven disciples went to Galilee, to the mountain
where Jesus had told them to go. 17 When they saw him, they worshiped
him; but some doubted. 18 Then Jesus came to them and said, "All
authority in heaven and on earth has been given to me. 19 Therefore go and
make disciples of all nations, baptizing them in the name of the Father and
of the Son and of the Holy Spirit, 20 and teaching them to obey everything
I have commanded you. And surely I am with you always, to the very end
of the age.

THE SMALL DETAILS

"For I am alive in you. See My presence in the small details of your life, the tiny miracles that are occurring every second of your existence. You breathe in and out. Your eyes see the world. You find a parking space. You exchange a look with a stranger that says more than a thousand words ever could.

"I reveal My presence to you in a million ways but you must have eyes to see. The scales no longer cloud your vision for you are a new creation in Christ. Stop taking this for granted! For you have work to do in Me and for Me. You are My hands and feet linked together as the body of Christ and bound together because of Me. Worship and adore Me, the one true God, your Lord Jesus Christ who died for you that you may be given new life.

"Come from an understanding that your life is a miracle, a priceless work of art fashioned by the Master Creator, freed from sin's slavery and redeemed through grace, out of the enemy's clutches forevermore, walking through this world and on towards eternity with your Heavenly Father.

"Realize all has been done for you and then do your very best for your Lord and for your fellow man. Love one another as you have been loved. Love the Lord your God with all your heart, soul, and mind.

"Think of us together in Eternity, as I have promised, every morning, and work backwards from there.

"Think of us together in Eternity, as I have promised, when you are being challenged. And take it from there."

Deuteronomy 6:5
Love the LORD your God with all your heart
and with all your soul and with all your strength.

Galatians 2:20
I have been crucified with Christ and I no longer live, but Christ lives in
me. The life I now live in the body, I live by faith in the Son of God, who
loved me and gave himself for me.

REFLECTION:
LET GO INTO THE
FULLNESS OF HIS GRACE

I see Jesus on the donkey on His way to Jerusalem, being exalted by the crowds. It is a polar opposite picture to what was to come. Jesus knew all that lay in store for Him. As believers, we too know what lies in store for us—Eternity with Jesus. And, knowing this, we live our lives in a way that honors that glorious gift: The gift of spending eternity with Jesus.

Yet the gift that precedes this is the gift of salvation at the Cross, with our sin being nailed to the Cross with Lord Jesus. And though we live in the fallen world and we cannot know what in this fallen world lies ahead, what we do know are the promises of God and His faithfulness to bring us through despite any circumstance that we are faced with. For all is illusion save the beauty and unsurpassed might of our precious Savior.

When we fix our eyes on His beautiful and wonderful face, and allow the fallen world to fall away, we look with an eternal perspective, we look on the One who set us free and who is vaster than we could imagine. The Lord of the Universe is for us! Who can be against us? What can come against us that does not pale in comparison to His goodness and grace and unending servant love for His redeemed children?

And as we live and step out in faith on the journey with Jesus, we yield to His commands, we wait obediently for His instructions, and for the Holy Spirit to reveal that which is hidden from our earthly eyes. Life becomes a letting go into the fullness of His grace. There is nothing sweeter than being loved by Jesus—our perfect Majestic Savior. His plan for us is perfect.

So we trust Him, we obey Him, we worship Him, we pray and listen to Him, we praise His name endlessly—in all circumstances. We ask for all that we lack to be made whole in Him. For His strength and His majesty lifts us higher than we could ever deserve or hope for. Our Redeemer.

Our Lord Jesus Christ! Praise Him!

> *Zechariah 4:6*
> *So he said to me, "This is the word of the LORD to Zerubbabel: 'Not by might nor by power,*
> *but by my Spirit,' says the LORD Almighty.*

> *Colossians 3:1*
> *Since, then, you have been raised with Christ, set your hearts on things above, where Christ is, seated at the right hand of God. 2 Set your minds on things above, not on earthly things. 3 For you died, and your life is now hidden with Christ in God. 4 When Christ, who is your life, appears, then you also will appear with him in glory.*

SECTION 6

NO SURPRISES

"There is nothing under Heaven that I do not know about. I know all that is to happen, has happened, and is happening. So there are no surprises for Me. And there are no surprises for you if you read My Scriptures carefully and faithfully and listen to the guidance through the provision of My Holy Spirit.

"You have all you need to walk with Me in accordance to My will. I have created a beautiful world for you. Walk in it, be amongst nature and see how unique each of My creations is. No two trees are the same, no two flowers; there is always a subtle difference between them. And you, My precious child, are My unique creation too, formed fearfully and wonderfully. I know the number of hairs on your head and I know the footsteps and the way you will tread before you take even one. And before you are there, I am there waiting for you.

"Be faithful, obey and trust, and allow My will to flow through you. Surrender to Me. Lose your life and you will gain your life. Come alongside Me and walk with Me. At times I will carry you if this is what is needed. I know what you need, I know who you are, I know where you are going. Trust in Me."

> *Deuteronomy 8:6*
> *Observe the commands of the LORD your God,*
> *walking in obedience to him and revering him.*

> *Matthew 10:39*
> *Whoever finds their life will lose it,*
> *and whoever loses their life for my sake will find it.*

RELY ON JESUS

"I am the true source of power. The great I Am. You can always find a way to be in My presence, and it is not always according to a formula that you attach yourself to at all costs. My dearest child, I am real, I am here, I am yours. You belong to Me.

"You are being refined like silver through a furnace and it is, as you have acknowledged, terrifying to have to rely on Me when you would rather be in control yourself. I have My ways and they are higher and broader than your own. When you come through the furnace and look back on what has been learned and applied, you then realize who I am in your life. Do not despair—believe Me when I say that you will never walk alone.

"Cling to Me and bloom through Me in adversity, when conditions are bitter and all seems bleak and desolate. When it is as though I have deserted you or I am not here for you, My promise to you is that I *am* here, no matter what.

"I am the God of transformation and I am transforming you bit by bit, little by little, step by step, moment by moment. You are not aware of this transformation at so many times because to you it feels murky and uncomfortable. Remember your feelings are transient and they will change literally like the wind. But your faith is the underpinning foundation to your life and you stand fast and firm on the rock that I Am.

"You commune with Me in safety and sanctuary, represented by this garden, and then you take up your Cross and you follow Me out into the world. Walk with Me and be alert. Be ready and willing to do all that I require in My Holy name. My love for you is unending and faithful. Remember this."

Isaiah 55:9

As the heavens are higher than the earth, so are my ways higher than your ways and my thoughts than your thoughts. 10 As the rain and the snow come down from heaven, and do not return to it without watering the earth and making it bud and flourish, so that it yields seed for the sower and bread for the eater, 11 so is my word that goes out from my mouth: It will not return to me empty, but will accomplish what I desire and achieve the purpose for which I sent it.

Matthew 16:24

Then Jesus said to his disciples, "Whoever wants to be my disciple must deny themselves and take up their Cross and follow me. 25 For whoever wants to save their life will lose it, but whoever loses their life for me will find it. 26 What good will it be for someone to gain the whole world, yet forfeit their soul? Or what can anyone give in exchange for their soul? 27 For the Son of Man is going to come in his Father's glory with his angels, and then he will reward each person according to what they have done.

"The race is not yet run. There is much to continue on with. Some days are seen by you as wasted, but I say to you, nothing is wasted; all can be used to encourage others and to glorify Me. The hardships and challenges, the mundaneness of daily life, are all part of living with faith.

"You are to fix your eyes on Me and trust in Me, knowing that I have promised and I will deliver. Go to Scripture—it is all there. Invite My Holy Spirit to reside in you—He is your guide each moment of your day. Pray and fast where necessary. Be with other believers. Walk in the world and be My light in the darkness.

"Encourage others. Love others. Do for others. Dwell in Me while looking outward at others. Do not be discouraged. Cheer up! I have overcome the world. And My Holy Spirit guides you to overcome. In My name."

> *1 Corinthians 9:24*
> *Do you not know that in a race all the runners run, but only one gets the prize? Run in such a way as to get the prize.*

> *Acts 4:31*
> *After they prayed, the place where they were meeting was shaken. And they were all filled with the Holy Spirit and spoke the word of God boldly.*

LIFE ABUNDANT

"Cast all your cares on Me and, once you do this, think of being with Me in Paradise. That is the promise I want you to concentrate on.

"Yet the enemy of this world, the father of lies, seeks for you to drown in the cares of this world. He wants you to focus on discord, doubt, despair, distress, desire, desperation, depression, and disharmony. He wants you to believe your cares are real and concrete. And well it may *appear* that these cares are real.

"Yet I have given you My promise that I will take care of you always. Just as I take care of the smallest of creatures, I have given you My promise that I have come to give you life, and life abundantly. I have promised never to forsake you. Yet you must lean not on your own understanding but fix your eyes on Me. To overcome your cares, remember I have overcome the world and fix your eyes on Me. I did not give you a spirit of fear. I expect boldness from you because I am a God of miracles, of transformation. I offer you forgiveness, a life lived in grace, and eternal life with Me in Paradise. All has been done for you.

"So whatever you do in My name, stand firm in My promises. I have made you aware that you will face persecution and hatred in My name—yet this too is part of My promise to you. These are also part of the cares that I want you to cast on Me.

"Look to those in My Holy Scriptures who were overcomers because of Me—David, Abraham, Joseph, Daniel, Gideon, Paul, Peter, Ruth, and Esther, to name a few—and know that you too are an overcomer because of Me.

"The truth of everyone and everything that is, is found in Me. Be free in Me and rest in Me. I am the way, the truth, and the life, I am the Kingdom, the power, and the glory, forever and ever. Amen."

> *2 Timothy 1:7*
> *For the Spirit God gave us does not make us timid, but gives us power, love and self-discipline.*

TURNING EVIL TO GOOD

"You were lost, now you are found. You cry for what you see as wasted time in your life. Yet there is no waste—for I am able to turn all that was for evil to good, and I am able to restore all that was lost. Yet cry your tears, My child, for your tears are what will help release you from the shackles of your past.

"And remember My promise that I shall wipe away every tear when we meet again. I am risen and alive in you today, tomorrow, and until we meet again face to face on that glorious day. Hallelujah!! Sing My praises, I who am your deliverer; you who can overcome with My strength.

"All things are possible within and with Me. So turn your face upwards and feel the warmth of My created sun on your face, feel the gentle breeze that I spoke into being, savor the fragrance of My handiwork— the flowers that surround you—and experience the lushness of the rich and silky grass beneath you that I made.

"Be in this sacred garden with Me for a while. No words needed, just time and space with Me, listening for My voice, being in My presence. Let your soul be refreshed and replenished, knowing that I Am."

> *Job 42:10*
> *After Job had prayed for his friends, the LORD restored his fortunes and gave him twice as much as he had before.*

> *Psalm 18:1*
> *I love you, LORD, my strength.*
> *2 The LORD is my rock, my fortress and my deliverer;*

MEREDITH SWIFT

my God is my rock, in whom I take refuge.
my shield and the horn of my salvation, my stronghold.

DISABILITY?

"Ponder on the miracle of creation, the miracle of the human body that I have formed. The intricacy of the design of eyes which see and perceive. The wonders of the mechanism of hands. How blood is circulated throughout the body. How each brain is wired for thinking. How each heart is a focal point for the body physically, and also has the capacity to love and experience being loved.

"Bodies can appear disabled, hands can be lost or not grow properly in the first place, there can be intellectual disabilities, sensory disabilities, other disabilities. Look beyond what is a seeming "disability" and how I am accessible to all, no matter whether they are in a "normal" functioning, fully intact body or not, no matter whether they are mentally ill or emotionally disturbed—all are My creations, all may come to Me and be fulfilled in Me.

"I have a plan for every single life that I created, which brings Me glory. I do not make mistakes. My intricate plan for all of creation is that they know Me and come to Me and glorify Me. Look again at My promises and you will find reasons and answers as to the "why" and "how" of My creations.

"The least becomes the greatest.

"Follow Me."

> *Exodus 4:11*
> *The LORD said to him, "Who gave human beings their mouths? Who makes them deaf or mute? Who gives them sight or makes them blind? Is it not I, the LORD?*

REFLECTION:
THE MASTERPIECE
OF ETERNITY

There is a mansion in Heaven, with rooms that are being prepared for me when my race is run. To know that there is a beautiful new place waiting for me, in a Heaven filled with heroes of faith and hopefully some of my closest loved ones, fills me with encouragement and anticipation. It helps me realize that my journey on earth is only a small part of a huge bigger picture. A masterpiece where Jesus and I get to spend Eternity together with the angels and our Heavenly Father in a place so indescribably perfect it will make everything brand new again.

What will it be like? I will have a new body, and I imagine I will have all my favorite things—my favorite food, the ideal home, the clothes that I would like to wear, and a life of constant, endless worship and praise adoring Jesus without the push and pull of earthly endeavours.

I can see vivid colors, a panorama of moving and vibrating multi-dimensional everything, fields of lush grass and a city of shining gold. It is breathtaking in its beauty. Yet most beautiful of all is Jesus. His robe is of radiant white—purer white than the softest of snow and fluffiest of clouds, His face radiant and shining and joyous. There is no time here in Heaven and I have a sense of just being totally in the moment, transfixed by the wonder of all that is around me.

There are thousands upon thousands of voices singing praises to the One who created them. I am part of the most angelic choir ever formed, part of the most magnificent place ever imagined, and I am to think of being here with Jesus in Eternity when I am feeling distracted and aimless.

I am to stop, breathe in my Lord Jesus' name, ask Him to come, and be still and wait to receive His presence. I am to think of being in this beautiful Heavenly abode with Him forever, knowing that my struggle is over and my race is run. I am to give thanks for the life I lead while I live on Earth and give thanks for the gift of eternal and precious life I have been given, knowing that every moment of this life counts, and that the enemy seeks to steal these moments by distracting me and giving me a restlessness of spirit that is not of my Lord Jesus. I am to refocus on Jesus and allow Him to lead my way again. Distraction is a perfect opportunity for praise and worship, reading the Scriptures, saying a prayer of thanksgiving for all that I have and all that the Lord has blessed me with.

As usual, my precious Savior, you rescue me from what I perceive to be wasted time. I re-focus on you and allow Your strength of purpose to refresh me and fill me again. Thank You, Jesus!

> *1 Corinthians 13:12*
> *For now we see only a reflection as in a mirror; then we shall see face to face. Now I know in part; then I shall know fully, even as I am fully known.*

> *Revelation 7:15*
> *Therefore, they are before the throne of God and serve him day and night in his temple; and he who sits on the throne will shelter them with his presence.*

SECTION 7

WALKING BY FAITH

"Darkness always follows the light of day—this is the natural order of things. And so you will find—when you have been through a particularly encouraging walk with Me, or a season of bounty and blessing—that there will be a time of darkness, where it may even seem that I have forsaken you. You have heard that these are the times when I carry you and they are also the times when you build your faith even stronger.

"You walk by faith as a human inhabiting and created to be in this world. You meet Me not as a fleshly human but rather a spirit-filled one. You rely on the Scriptures, your prayers, your times of quiet when you are listening for My voice, the Holy Spirit, and your own personal revelation of Me to give you the relationship with Me that I require. You do not see Me with your eyes, you see Me with your heart, your soul, and your mind, and this is how you are to love Me also.

"For I am your God and you are My child, I am your Jesus and you are My precious one, I am Your Savior who gave up My life willingly and knowingly, so that I could be in relationship with you and so that this bond would sustain until we are able to meet face to face again on that glorious day when I come for you.

"Do not be discouraged about the darkness, My child, but know that I am with you and continue your walk with Me in faith."

2 Corinthians 5:7
For we live by faith, not by sight.

Hebrews 13:5

Keep your lives free from the love of money and be content with what you have, because God has said, "Never will I leave you; never will I forsake you." 6 So we say with confidence, "The Lord is my helper; I will not be afraid. What can mere mortals do to me?"

SAVED BY GRACE

"I have shown the way to come to My Father. I am the way. No one comes to the Father except through Me.

"My instructions are clear to you - 'Love the Lord your God with all your heart, soul, and mind,' and, 'Love one another as I have loved you.' Yet these instructions, profoundly simple as they are, are also profoundly challenging for man in this fallen world.

"Your fallen nature makes you do that which you do not want to do, that which you wished you had not done, that which you know you should not have done. Yet after each poor choice, genuinely repent and continue on, continue striving, following Me, onwards and upwards and towards the prize of living with Me in Paradise forever.

"You have been created in My image, you have been saved by grace, forgiven of all of your sin. I became that sin, and you were washed clean and pure and dazzlingly white as fresh fallen snow. My blood covered your sin. I paid the price.

"Now in relationship with Me, your price is living the way My followers are required and challenged to live. This is not an easy challenge, but the rewards are immeasurable. So be of good cheer and continue—onwards and upwards—towards Me."

> *Isaiah 1:18*
> *"Come now, let us settle the matter," says the LORD. "Though your sins are like scarlet, they shall be as white as snow; though they are red as crimson, they shall be like wool."*

MEREDITH SWIFT

1 Peter 1:3

Praise be to the God and Father of our Lord Jesus Christ!
In his great mercy he has given us new birth into a living hope through the
resurrection of Jesus Christ from the dead, 4 and into an inheritance that
can never perish, spoil or fade. This inheritance is kept in heaven for you, 5
who through faith are shielded by God's power until the coming of the
salvation that is ready to be revealed in the last time. 6 In all this you
greatly rejoice, though now for a little while you may have had to suffer grief
in all kinds of trials.

YOUR STORY

"I knew you before you were born; you cannot imagine how lovingly I created you! I worked out what your physical features would be, I designed your family, where you would be born, what you would experience.

"I fashioned you into magnificence and breathed you into being. I formulated a plan for your life, gave you strength of character and a soft and tender heart.

"I created challenges along the way and I protected you. All through your life I protected you from the enemy. He could not have you. I knew when and where you would finally give your heart to Me. And oh, the rejoicing in Heaven when this happened!!!

"And I know all of the rest of your story too, My precious child, from beginning to middle to end. It is a wondrous story of redemption and restoration. So do not despair, precious one—because I know who you are, from the top of your head to the tips of your toes and from the depths of your heart, I know who you are. You are Mine!!!! Always.

"So step joyfully into each day, knowing that your purpose is great and glorifying to Me. I love you!"

> *Psalm 139:13*
> *For you created my inmost being;*
> *you knit me together in my mother's womb.*
> *14 I praise you because I am fearfully and wonderfully made;*
> *your works are wonderful,*
> *I know that full well.*
> *15 My frame was not hidden from you*

when I was made in the secret place,
when I was woven together in the depths of the earth.
16 Your eyes saw my unformed body;
all the days ordained for me were written in your book
before one of them came to be.

Jeremiah 1:4
The word of the LORD came to me, saying,
5 "Before I formed you in the womb I knew you,
before you were born I set you apart;
I appointed you as a prophet to the nations."

TIMES OF REPLENISHMENT

"Times of replenishment in Me are mandatory. Times where you listen for My word, where you pray, you fast, you immerse yourself in Scripture, where you meet with other believers, and where you spend time with those you love and care for.

"Times where the busyness and business of the world are set aside and you honor Me by resting. This is Biblical. I rested on the seventh day of My creation of the world.

"Built within all of My creations is the need for resting and rejuvenation. So realize that this stillness and contemplation time is not an option, it is an essential."

> *Leviticus 23:3*
> *"There are six days when you may work, but the seventh day is a day of sabbath rest, a day of sacred assembly. You are not to do any work; wherever you live, it is a sabbath to the Lord.*

> *Hebrews 4:4*
> *For somewhere he has spoken about the seventh day in these words: "On the seventh day God rested from all his works."*

DEPEND ABSOLUTELY . . .
ON JESUS!

"I like to walk closely with you and to carry you as often as you will allow Me. I encourage and insist on your absolute dependence on Me.

"Yet when you walk back into the natural fallen world the task becomes much more difficult. You often yearn for what My will is for your life. Are you doing enough? Are you doing what I am asking you to do, what My will for you is? Is your life as I would want it to be—for Me and through Me, every second?

"Resolve to walk so closely with Me that you are utterly dependent on Me. Allow yourself weakness and surrender your control, hand all to Me, give all to Me. Resolve to pray for My will more fervently, pray for My expansion on your life more fervently, pray for My blessing more fervently, pray for My hand to be on you, My dearest child, more fervently.

"Allow yourself to be vulnerable and open for Me, knowing that I am the source of all power and strength. Pray that you would be carried along in the supernatural flow of a life lived for Me and in Me, not knowing where I begin and where you end.

"This is your challenge, to take up your Cross and follow Me. For I am Your Savior who gave all as I hung on that Cross, I am your Lord of all, God of transformation, healer of the sick and the hope for the hopeless.

"Abide in Me."

> *Romans 12:1*
> *Therefore, I urge you, brothers and sisters, in view of God's mercy, to offer your bodies as a living sacrifice, holy and pleasing to God—this is your*

true and proper worship. 2 Do not conform to the pattern of this world, but be transformed by the renewing of your mind. Then you will be able to test and approve what God's will is—his good, pleasing and perfect will.

THE ANTIDOTE TO FEAR

"Walking on water, turning water into wine, feeding the 5000, raising the dead—rising from the dead!!! Have not the miracles of My ministry been recorded in My Scriptures? And the same power that is in Me and raised Me from the dead lives in you also.

"Yet fear is also inherent in the human condition, since the Fall of Adam and Eve into sin. And the two of these exist—the miracles of the Lord Jesus and the fear that is so much a part of humankind—side by side.

"What is the antidote? It is simple—put your attention onto that which shows you life and life abundant, rather than that which shrinks your existence into a tiny, worthless speck of dust.

"For that is what the enemy wishes for your life—that you do and will believe you are insignificant and worthless, fearful and wary. But My plan for you is magnificent and I came to set you free from all the doubts and worries, all the shackles that the enemy would have you believe are real. They are not!

"Pray for largeness—open your mouth wide and accept that I Am, that I am alive, and I am coming back. Pray for largeness so that you may fulfil your part in the Great Commission. Pray for boldness, pray for huge revival.

"And repent of all your wrongdoing, repent sincerely, and empty out your heart of any sin or unforgiveness that resides therein. Come before Me and My throne of grace—for I hold out My arms to you, I shower you with the grace that is now your hope—and which My blood poured out on the Cross paid in full for. I came for *you*. Believe this!"

HEARING HIS VOICE

Psalm 81:10
I am the Lord your God,
who brought you up out of Egypt.
Open wide your mouth and I will fill it.

2 Corinthians 3:11
And if what was transitory came with glory, how much greater is the glory
of that which lasts! 12 Therefore, since we have such a hope, we are very
bold.

REFLECTION:
THE PROMISE OF REDEMPTION, TRANSFORMATION AND JOY

I feel completely nurtured and bathed in the presence of Jesus' love when I am in this Garden of Promise. I call it the Garden of Promise because my Jesus meets me here. And He is my Promise.

He is my Promise of redemption, of transformation, of joy. He is my Promise that every one of my tears shall be wiped away on that glorious day when we meet face to face. He is my Promise that nothing can break our bond now that I belong to Him; now that I have chosen for Him to live inside my heart. He is my Promise through His Holy Spirit that He will guide me all of my days. He is my Promise that He will be glorified through me with the work He has created and anointed me for. He is my Promise that I will never again walk alone. He is my Promise of salvation!

My precious Savior, the Lord Jesus Christ—faithful, loyal and abiding, living within me and imbuing me with His richness of purpose and sureness of step because He has forgiven me and saved me—completely and utterly.

Jesus is my Promise and I have a promise for Him too—a promise to listen for His voice, a promise to obey His voice, a promise to apply whatever instructions His voice gives me. His beautiful voice—still and small, yet unimaginable in its might and ability to speak all of creation into being. His voice—speaking and breathing new life into me with His Holy Spirit. His voice—pure love, drenched with living water and redemptive grace. His voice—the voice of righteous truth and fiery perfection.

I could never have imagined in my wildest dreams the journey I am on with Jesus. Exciting, encouraging, and oh, so enormously challenging! A process of liberation and transformation, all stemming from one simple act on my behalf—accepting His offer to allow Him to live inside of my heart—and one profound act on His—dying on a Cross, taking on the sin of the world and then rising from the dead to live in relationship with me forever.

If you cannot accept Jesus into your heart, you will never know the richness of what He is offering you. You will never know His tender love and ability to totally and completely transform all that is broken and hurting inside you. You will never know the profoundness of journey and the plan He has to help you prosper and prepare you for eternal relationship with Him. Say yes to Jesus. Now. He is waiting for you. Not a minute to waste. Say yes now.

Galatians 3:26
So in Christ Jesus you are all children of God through faith, 27 for all of you who were baptized into Christ have clothed yourselves with Christ. 28 There is neither Jew nor Gentile, neither slave nor free, nor is there male and female, for you are all one in Christ Jesus. 29 If you belong to Christ, then you are Abraham's seed, and heirs according to the promise.

2 Peter 1:4
Through these he has given us his very great and precious promises, so that through them you may participate in the divine nature, having escaped the corruption in the world caused by evil desires.

SECTION 8

SINK INTO JESUS

"Rest in Me means sink into Me, dear precious child of Mine. It means keeping constant in Me, not allowing yourself to become distracted by the twists and turns of the earthly realm. The tone to your life is Me, the foundation to your life is Me.

"Do not allow yourself to become distracted—this is so easy for you to do; it is so easy for this to happen. The instant you take your eyes off Me the enemy can come in—can snatch a thought or plant a seed of doubt. These things happen so quickly.

"Sow your seed of trust deep within My love for you and it shall sprout safely and bear fruit. You don't need to know today where this will take you, what direction your life will go in, nor how I will shape this into My purposes for you—only trust in Me and allow Me to take your life and run with it in My strength, according to My will. Just keep your eyes on Me.

"Simple yet difficult, due to your fallen nature. And here is where trusting like a little child will serve you. The simplicity of a child's trust is where you want to head. Without the adult rationalizations of 'Should I? Shouldn't I? How? When? Where? Why? What?' No, dear child, simply trust like a child trusts.

"In Me. For Me. With Me. Always. I am waiting to serve you. Be with Me."

> Matthew 21:21
> Jesus replied, "Truly I tell you, if you have faith and do not doubt, not only can you do what was done to the fig tree, but also you can say to this mountain, 'Go, throw yourself into the sea,' and it will be done.

1 Corinthians 7:35
I am saying this for your own good, not to restrict you, but that you may live in a right way in undivided devotion to the Lord.

THE GREAT COMMISSION

"The harvest is great but the workers are few. In My name, labor less with your hands and more with your words—for your words can be either the weapons of death or the bringers of life. Choose wisely which one they will be.

"Remember that My Word created this world and all of the universes, all of creation. As you are part of My creation given the ability to speak, the natural flow on from this is that there is great power within your choice of words—the power to uplift and bring life and hope, or the power to tear down, discourage, and destroy.

"The Great Commission to spread my life-giving gospel is dependent mainly on your words. So ask the Holy Spirit to guide you to those who are earnestly seeking a hope that is eternal and share My message, in My name, with them.

"Be also of service to all that you meet in whichever way is possible for you. And again, ask for My help in this.

"Be spirit filled and open to the opportunity to share My gospel in whichever way you are able, and whenever you are able, yet also when you are feeling uncomfortable. Call on My assistance and I will give you the words you require. Abide with Me."

> *Ephesians 4:29*
> *Do not let any unwholesome talk come out of your mouths, but only what is helpful for building others up according to their needs, that it may benefit those who listen. 30 And do not grieve the Holy Spirit of God, with whom you were sealed for the day of redemption. 31 Get rid of all bitterness, rage*

and anger, brawling and slander, along with every form of malice. 32 Be kind and compassionate to one another, forgiving each other, just as in Christ God forgave you.

James 3:8
but no human being can tame the tongue. It is a restless evil, full of deadly poison. 9 With the tongue we praise our Lord and Father, and with it we curse human beings, who have been made in God's likeness. 10 Out of the same mouth come praise and cursing. My brothers and sisters, this should not be.

RELATIONSHIP WITH JESUS

"My precious child, I love you more than words can express to you. I will never forsake you, never abandon you. Trust in Me. Your life is a testimony to Me, for My glory. I guide your footsteps; I bring you through all the storms and sunshine moments of life. I am there for you as the rock solid foundation of a life that is so precious to Me.

"Fix your eyes on Me, know that you are loved truly and deeply. Let Me carry you when you are burdened, let Me take your burdens from you, let Me give you My strength when yours is gone. My yoke is light. Be with Me. Relax in Me. Rest in Me. Each day give yourself to Me afresh. Repent. Renew the promise of hope I gave you the day you gave your life to Me and I gave you new life; the day I set you free to be with Me forever and ever.

"Praise be to God you found the courage to accept Me. For I was unseen and largely unknown to you, I was a stirring within your heart, a still small whisper that urged you to come to Me. There was great fear before you accepted Me, placed into your mind by the enemy. Yet I had your heart and your heart is where I spoke to you from. Placing your faith in Me could have been seen as a risk, yet there was and is no risk with the relationship I offer you. It is rock solid, secure, and safe.

"Relationship with Me promises the ultimate happy-ever-after ending when you live with Me in Paradise. This life of yours is a precious gift, yet also a speck of dust, as it passes so quickly. Be faithful to My commandments, dear child, and each day renew My covenant with you. Keep your eyes on Me and I will guide you, uplift you, strengthen and encourage you. I love you. Always."

Jeremiah 31:3
The LORD appeared to us in the past, saying:
"I have loved you with an everlasting love;
I have drawn you with unfailing kindness.

2 Corinthians 5:17
Therefore, if anyone is in Christ, the new creation has come: The old has gone, the new is here! 18 All this is from God, who reconciled us to himself through Christ and gave us the ministry of reconciliation: 19 that God was reconciling the world to himself in Christ, not counting people's sins against them. And he has committed to us the message of reconciliation.

OVERCOMING IN JESUS

"As the overcomer of death, I offer you the help that allows you to be an overcomer of any challenges you face as you journey in your life. This overcoming help is also a transforming help. I give you all that you need in order to be an overcomer. So any challenges that you may face within your character—those parts of your character that need transforming—I can help you with. I can help you to overcome.

"But you must be willing to ask for this help and be willing to journey closely with Me and be obedient to My instructions as this help goes to work within you, guided by My Holy Spirit, to transform all that is darkness within you into light. It is My transforming aim to help you cultivate your character and grow all the fruits of the Spirit—love, joy, peace, forbearance, kindness, goodness, faithfulness, gentleness, and self-control. Ask Me to help you and I will. This will draw you closer to Me as you cultivate dependence on Me. I seek for you to be entirely dependent on Me.

"You can do all things if you allow Me to strengthen you. I am weeding your garden, pruning; getting rid of all that is not of Me. My living water will help your garden to bloom, My love and faithfulness will be as fertilizer to nourish your garden, and My Holy Spirit will give you all the instructions you need to know as to how your garden is to be tended."

> *John 15:1*
> *"I am the true vine, and my Father is the gardener. 2 He cuts off every branch in me that bears no fruit, while every branch that does bear fruit he prunes so that it will be even more fruitful. 3 You are already clean because*

of the word I have spoken to you. 4 Remain in me, as I also remain in you. No branch can bear fruit by itself; it must remain in the vine. Neither can you bear fruit unless you remain in me.

AT THE FOOT OF THE CROSS

"Just as I prune and cut back the vine so that it may bear more fruit, so too may you cut off in My name that which does not serve you—past and present circumstances, parts of your character, and also generational curses that have been part of your family within and without living memory.

"You are living a life I have given you which is cluttered by these curses. You do not see them, and the enemy in his deceit seeks to keep them hidden from you. The curses of illness and idolatry are especially prevalent. Ask that these be revealed to you in My mighty name and then take them to the foot of My Holy Cross. Ask that they be cut off in My mighty name and invite Me to inhabit the space where they used to reside within you. Ask that this be done for all generational curses. Each time you are able to do this in My name the enemy loses ground and you become stronger within Me. There is more room for the fruit of the Spirit to grow and develop.

"There is no fear to be attached to this process, rather an openness and willingness, knowing I am with you; knowing that you abide in Me. This is part of the process in gaining freedom as you journey with Me and as your life becomes more and more lived for Me. In My name always, pray for deliverance and healing. Enlist the help of your trusted brothers and sisters in Christ to pray for you always. When two or three are gathered in My name, I will be there. Go in peace now."

Numbers 14:18
The Lord is slow to anger, abounding in love and forgiving sin and rebellion. Yet he does not leave the guilty unpunished; he punishes the children for the sin of the parents to the third and fourth generation.'

Matthew 18:18

"Truly I tell you, whatever you bind on earth will be bound in heaven, and whatever you loose on earth will be loosed in heaven. 19 "Again, truly I tell you that if two of you on earth agree about anything they ask for, it will be done for them by my Father in heaven. 20 For where two or three gather in my name, there am I with them."

ROCK MY SOUL

"There are times when you need to treat yourself like a little tiny baby, worthy of the utmost in care and attention, trusting for your food and clothing and for your caregivers to love you and provide that nurturing sustenance.

"There are times when you do nothing but all is done for you. These are just such times for you, dear precious child. This is your time when you require that nurturing and to not be called upon to do extra nor to be anything other than who you completely are. That it is enough to just be.

"This is how I love you.

"All was done for you at the Cross.

"So rest in Me, letting yourself be rocked gently, safe in the knowledge of My everlasting love, knowing that you are more than enough. I love you."

> *1 John 4:7*
> *Dear friends, let us love one another, for love comes from God. Everyone who loves has been born of God and knows God.*

> *Ephesians 5:2*
> *and walk in the way of love, just as Christ loved us and gave himself up for us as a fragrant offering and sacrifice to God.*

REFLECTION:
IS YOUR HOUSE IN ORDER?

He is appearing in the clouds, on His white horse. Are you ready for Him? Is your house in order? Are you thinking you needed to have shared your faith, shared the gospel, more? Because Jesus is here!!! And you know you are going to be speaking to Him and you know you will be accountable to Him. You will be with Him—YES—and you want to make sure you will be able to make a favorable report. You want to hear Him say those wonderful words "Well done, good and faithful servant."

So we fix our eyes on and serve the one true King. We examine what "serve" actually means—loving one another and caring enough, in service, to share our faith. No man knows the time Jesus is coming back and no man needs to know. As we lift our eyes Heavenward and outstretch our hands to Jesus, let us remember to stretch our hands to our fellow man and woman with the good news of the gospel. He is risen! And He's coming back! So get ready—get set—go share your faith!

There will never be another moment like this one. Reach out, reach up, and reach mankind for Him. In the Holy and Mighty name of Jesus we pray the Holy Spirit will guide our footsteps and will prepare the way so that we may be the vessel by which the gospel is shared.

Dear Holy Spirit, guide us and place that one in front of us who is searching and seeking for truth. Equip us with the necessary words to touch hearts and transform lives in Your name, Jesus. Let the message be shared abundantly and all glory be to God!!!! Amen.

Matthew 24:42
"Therefore keep watch, because you do not know on what day your Lord

will come. 43 But understand this: If the owner of the house had known at what time of night the thief was coming, he would have kept watch and would not have let his house be broken into. 44 So you also must be ready, because the Son of Man will come at an hour when you do not expect him."

Acts 1:7

He said to them: "It is not for you to know the times or dates the Father has set by his own authority. 8 But you will receive power when the Holy Spirit comes on you; and you will be my witnesses in Jerusalem, and in all Judea and Samaria, and to the ends of the earth." 9 After he said this, he was taken up before their very eyes, and a cloud hid him from their sight. 10 They were looking intently up into the sky as he was going, when suddenly two men dressed in white stood beside them. 11 "Men of Galilee," they said, "why do you stand here looking into the sky? This same Jesus, who has been taken from you into heaven, will come back in the same way you have seen him go into heaven."

SECTION 9

SEEK FIRST THE
KINGDOM OF GOD

"There is man's way and God's way in all facets of the life you are living. Man's way seeks to control, make sense of, and work out all situations in his own strength. Man's way is to be in the driver's seat always, exalting the self and taking the credit for all good, or feeling completely overwhelmed when the bad occurs. And the bad will occur, because this is a fallen world.

"Seek first the Kingdom of God, acknowledging that I am in control. Surrender and live in obedience to My will, lean not on your own understanding and acknowledge that I have a plan and purpose for your life. I am the overseer and author of your life and you are to give Me full and utmost glory.

"Choose not to become attached to feelings or circumstances but rather fix your eyes on Me, your Creator, the one true God, and allow Me to guide you, shape you, carry you, and love you. Prayer and thanksgiving will keep you close to Me. Listen for My voice, fast, read My Scriptures, and repent daily. Refresh and renew your spirit as you walk ever more closely with Me. Let Me satisfy your spiritual hunger and quench your spiritual thirst with My living water.

"This is a personal relationship that we share, and the more you communicate with Me, the more this relationship will deepen and the more it will enrich and transform all facets of your life. I am the God of transformation. You are My child and I am your God. Know this and live accordingly. I love you, My dearest, precious, fragile child. Depend on Me. Unlike fallen man, I am perfect and completely faithful, the spotless Lamb who sacrificed willingly to enter into a relationship with you, to free you from sin's bondage, and to bring you Home at the end of your life's journey.

"Abide with Me."

> *Matthew 6:33*
> *But seek first his kingdom and his righteousness,*
> *and all these things will be given to you as well.*

> *2 Corinthians 6:18*
> *And, "I will be a Father to you, and you will be my sons and daughters,*
> *says the Lord Almighty."*

THE POWER OF JESUS

"Be aware of the beautiful world I have created for you! The beauty of nature, the softness of the breeze, the majesty of the trees, the gentle warmth of a soothing sun. The quietness of nature. The diversity of nature. Each part of nature completely unique yet each part of a glorious whole. Order runs throughout the whole of nature and throughout the whole of My creation.

"In this time you find yourself in an age where there is much automation and information, and this can be troubling and disorderly to your spirit. Seek nature as a balance to this. And seek Me as the antidote to this, the true and perfect antidote, so that no matter what you encounter, no matter what troubles your spirit or makes you restless or unsettled, that I am an anchor to bring you back to what is truly real.

"I am the only reality in this life for you—all else is an illusion. You are in preparation for the time to come when you will spend Eternity with Me. Be in the world but not of it. Be the overcomer whose only place and purpose in this world is to reflect My glory and spread the message of hope of My unchanging gospel.

"I Am the great I Am, your God of power and might and authority, who can move mountains; who brought the stars into being, all with My Word. Read My Word, cultivate your relationship with Me, be with Me and let Me give you the love and assurance I promise in My Holy Scriptures."

Psalm 23
1 The Lord is my shepherd, I lack nothing.
2 He makes me lie down in green pastures,
he leads me beside quiet waters,

3 he refreshes my soul.
He guides me along the right paths
for his name's sake.
4 Even though I walk
through the darkest valley, I will fear no evil,
for you are with me;
your rod and your staff,
they comfort me.
5 You prepare a table before me
in the presence of my enemies.
You anoint my head with oil;
my cup overflows.
6 Surely your goodness and love will follow me
all the days of my life,
and I will dwell in the house of the Lord
forever.

WILLINGNESS WITH JESUS

"Be of willingness, dear child. Willing to seek Me. Willing to do for Me. Willing to be My hands and feet in the many different ways there are to serve your fellow man. Willing to have an open heart and ears to listen and eyes that see. Willing to stand up for Me and spread My message of hope.

"This is not always easy. Willingness is wanting to do what I will for you to do. I know the plan I have for you, dear child. I have all the pieces of the puzzle. And I hold them, and I hold you, in the palm of My hand. Know this at the deepest level of your being. That I hold you in the palm of My hand, My precious child. No matter what is required of you to do, in My name, I have you in the palm of My hand. And that is strength for you. It is encouragement. It is might. It is power.

"Yet you cannot be aware of this, living in your fleshly body and with your fallen nature. Here is where your faith comes in. Faith in Me. Faith in My Holy Spirit to guide you and instruct you. Faith in My Scriptures as My Word to you. Faith in My gospel of hope. Faith in the love I hold for you always. The unseen and the unknown is made clear because of My message of hope and for My provision of deliverance, through the promise of redemption and the price that was paid to pay the debt in full at the Cross.

"So stand tall, walk in confidence, and be of good cheer, My overcoming, most precious child. I am yours and you are Mine—always, until the end of this world. And on that day when your breath leaves your body and I am instantly there to take you Home you will see in all My glory the wondrous plan that I fashioned for your life.

"Until then, trust in Me. Abide in Me. Go in peace. I love you."

Luke 22:41

He withdrew about a stone's throw beyond them, knelt down and prayed, 42 "Father, if you are willing, take this cup from me; yet not my will, but yours be done." 43 An angel from heaven appeared to him and strengthened him. 44 And being in anguish, he prayed more earnestly, and his sweat was like drops of blood falling to the ground.

2 Corinthians 8:12

For if the willingness is there, the gift is acceptable according to what one has, not according to what one does not have.

GROWING IN FAITH

"I am the light of the world, that which can be seen clearly, but you must have eyes to see.

"I awaken your spiritual eyes when you give your heart to Me and My Holy Spirit is allowed to come into you. You are born again, like a newborn little baby, precious, innocent, and pure. Just as when a baby is born it cannot be given solid food and needs the milk from its mother, so too must you as a new life within Me be given nurture and support and the opportunity to become well-grounded in your new faith and in your new life.

"Yet you must also grow, and as you grow, step by step, the journey with Me becomes more challenging. You must grow beyond the milk and onto the meat. This is accomplished through the deepening of the relationship with Me. It unfolds.

"Your service becomes more, your focus on yourself becomes less, your prayer life becomes deeper, your worries loosen their hold over you. Yet still I am always there with you. To uplift you, guide you, encourage you, nurture you, and be with you as you develop your gifts and your service to others.

"Do not doubt the journey I have you on, My precious child. Do not be afraid to go deeper. Each day as you go deeper in Me, you will find you die to self more, you will find you live for Me more, you will find joy as you are liberated from the bondage of being determined and defined by your circumstances.

"So lean not on your own understanding, but instead, delight in My promises. For I am faithful, unending, unyielding, and Sovereign in the

Plan I have for you. Rest in the knowledge I am the same today, tomorrow, and yesterday. I am your deliverer, the voice of your Shepherd, My darling, most precious little sheep. I set you free the moment I entered your heart. Now be with Me."

Isaiah 40:11
He tends his flock like a shepherd:
He gathers the lambs in his arms
and carries them close to his heart;
he gently leads those that have young.

Ephesians 1:18
I pray that the eyes of your heart may be enlightened in order that you may know the hope to which he has called you, the riches of his glorious inheritance in his holy people.

RESTORING EQUILIBRIUM

"More and more, this world is seen to be an illusion, dear child. More and more, as your relationship with Me deepens, the things of this world lose their appeal. More and more, the desire to be obedient to My will and dependent on Me is the only thing that matters. This is what is meant by losing your life to find it.

"Before you gave your heart to Me you were a child seeded from Adam. Yet from the moment you became Mine you were born into a new bloodline and a new seed was planted within you. This seed is the seed of My promises, of new life, hope eternal, and a richness of journey such that you could never have imagined nor previously experienced.

"When you look back at your old life you can see that you were asleep. Now you have awakened and the new day has dawned. The old things have passed away and lost their meaning; you walk through this world as a stranger in it but not of it.

"Yet there is no need for isolation within this. As you realize more and more your purpose and the reason why you were created, there is a joy that bubbles up within you, a serenity and a security unlike any other. As the fruit of the Spirit become cultivated within you and you make the choice each day to journey closely with Me, and the teachings and truth conveyed in My Holy Scripture, you become aware of the indwelling of My Holy Spirit and the limitless source of power that exists to you as a precious and sanctified child of God.

"Be bold as you bring My message of hope to this lost and hurting world. Let Me guide and support you in all that this entails, My chosen and cherished precious one. Let not your spirit be troubled as I am with you always. Peace be with you."

Deuteronomy 10:20
Fear the LORD your God and serve him. Hold fast to him and take your
oaths in his name. 21 He is the one you praise; he is your God, who
performed for you those great and awesome wonders you saw with your own
eyes.

Psalm 138:1
I will praise you, LORD, with all my heart;
before the "gods" I will sing your praise.
2 I will bow down toward your holy temple
and will praise your name
for your unfailing love and your faithfulness,
for you have so exalted your solemn decree
that it surpasses your fame.
3 When I called, you answered me;
you greatly emboldened me.

WALKING WITH JESUS

"Born unto Me, a new creation in Me, sanctified by Me and justified by Me. You are Mine, you belong to Me and with Me now. Your body and your spirit are in My tender care now, and I seek to lavish infinite attention and love on you.

"I ask only that you cultivate a relationship with Me, a willingness to grow deeper in My love and in Me every day of your life. And I ask that you break this down into hour by hour, further down into minute by minute, still further down into second by second. So that My Holy Spirit is a constant guide to you and I am in constant communication with you. Your spiritual walk with Me will thus be run parallel to your physical walk on the earth.

"Life with Me goes from one-dimensional black and white to multi-dimensional living, breathing, vivid color. There is shade and texture in relationship with Me where before there was only plainness and sameness. This is because My living water is the only thing that can satisfy you at your deepest level of your being. I created you this way and the longing you feel within the deepest fibers of your being can only be met and satisfied through Me.

"Place Me first always in all that you think, say, and do. You no longer walk alone. My greatest desire is for relationship with you, communion with you, for My glorification through you.

"I have designed you intricately, gifted you, and mapped out a journey for you. Now that you realize and know that I am with you every step of that journey there is a richness and purpose and meaning to all that you do. Work with Me on this.

"There is blessing and joy in all circumstances because of what I have done for you at the Cross and because I am always with you. I have forgiven you of all of your sin, past, present, and future. I have washed you clean with My spilled blood. I have sanctified you and raised you up into royalty with your agreement to allow Me to enter into your precious heart.

"Let Me continue to guide you, to be with you, to be in that intimacy of relationship with you. I earnestly seek your company and your praise and thanksgiving. Abide with Me."

> *1 Corinthians 6:11*
> *And that is what some of you were. But you were washed, you were sanctified, you were justified in the name of the Lord Jesus Christ and by the Spirit of our God.*

> *Titus 3:3*
> *At one time we too were foolish, disobedient, deceived and enslaved by all kinds of passions and pleasures. We lived in malice and envy, being hated and hating one another. 4 But when the kindness and love of God our Savior appeared, he saved us, 5 not because of righteous things we had done, but because of his mercy. He saved us through the washing of rebirth and renewal by the Holy Spirit.*

REFLECTION:
PRAISING THE ONE
WHO MADE ME!

I lift my arms up to praise the One who made me. I lift my arms up to worship Him and to thank Him for all the blessings He has given me. I lift my arms up to praise Him for every part of my life—for the suffering, the hardship, the beauty, the joy, the not knowing of Him and the knowing of Him. I am grateful and humbled to be right here, safe in my Savior's loving embrace, with my heart ready and waiting for the next part of my journey with Him.

I have known what it is to not know my Creator and, compared to now, it was a dull, colorless, and reactive existence. Now my world is viewed through the lens of the One who set me free; a radically altered shift in every part of me.

I serve You, Jesus, as best I can, though sometimes I am kicking and screaming not to do what You need me to do. Sometimes Your still, small voice has to repeat the same thing quite a few times before I pay attention. Yet You are patient, faithful, and gentle with my disobedient ways. I think that is because You have my heart and You know I belong to You.

Let me stay in Your Presence forever, Lord, being with You and being for You. Let my actions bring glory to You and let me not be lacking in having my heart set on course for You, Jesus. Let it all be for you, Lord. There is no one else but You.

I praise You!

Deuteronomy 28:2
All these blessings will come on you and accompany you if you obey the Lord your God.

Luke 6:46
"Why do you call me, 'Lord, Lord,' and do not do what I say? 47 As for everyone who comes to me and hears my words and puts them into practice, I will show you what they are like. 48 They are like a man building a house, who dug down deep and laid the foundation on rock. When a flood came, the torrent struck that house but could not shake it, because it was well built. 49 But the one who hears my words and does not put them into practice is like a man who built a house on the ground without a foundation. The moment the torrent struck that house, it collapsed and its destruction was complete."

SECTION 10

SNAP! SNAP! SNAP!

"Your feelings come and go—snap, snap, snap! Do not mistake them for anything more than transitory parts of your humanness. They assist you to process the events of your daily life, but they must not be seen to be an anchoring point in your daily life. They are not to be trusted the way I am to be trusted. So don't become attached to them or act only on them, just allow them to flow freely throughout your body.

"Faith and trust in Me, obedience to Me, listening for My voice, praying to and worshiping Me—these are to be the anchors for your life. When you are restless and fragmented by your feelings this is an indicator that it is a time to be still, get quiet, and surrender to My rest and peace. The restlessness in your spirit is the work of the enemy. Take time out. Immediately.

"Stop all outer distractions and turn inward. Ask for My help and guidance to be revealed through the Holy Spirit as you read My Scriptures. I will put all your pieces back together again. I will soothe and uplift you in your brokenness until you are able to feel whole in Me again. Only take the time for Me and for this to be so. And in perfect time it shall be.

"Sometimes there is a season of waiting where a season of patience is required; waiting on My will for a direction you may want to go in. But know this, My most precious and treasured child, I will open only those doors which are for your ultimate good and firmly shut those which are of the enemy. And My timing is perfect. Never doubt this.

"Trust and obey Me, safe in the knowledge that I have a good Plan for your life and all that I have for you is for your good and My glory. I am faithful. I am merciful. I have been where you are. Trust in Me. Take time for Me. Rest and refresh yourself in Me."

Psalm 27:13
I remain confident of this:
I will see the goodness of the LORD
in the land of the living.
14 Wait for the LORD;
be strong and take heart
and wait for the LORD.

Colossians 1:15
The Son is the image of the invisible God, the firstborn over all creation. 16
For in him all things were created: things in heaven and on earth, visible
and invisible, whether thrones or powers or rulers or authorities; all things
have been created through him and for him. 17 He is before all things, and
in him all things hold together.

HEALING THE
BROKEN-HEARTED

"I came to heal the broken-hearted, softening and remodeling them, stripping away all that was old and stale. I came for the sick, not the well. I came for the sinners, not those who are righteous. I came to give hope in a lost and hurting world, breathing fresh hope and promise into it with My Holy Spirit and the majesty of My Creator's voice and hands.

"My love is unfailing and never changes. I am the same yesterday, today, and tomorrow. My sacrifice has allowed all those enslaved by the crushing weight of their multitude of sins to be freed of their burdens, their sins lifted and completely forgotten about as I cast the memory of them far away where I remember them no longer. I am no longer interested in them. They are gone.

"It is finished. I came to claim as many of My children as are willing to turn to Me, who are willing to allow their hard hearts to be softened, who are willing to lay aside their logical reasoning and to trust in Me and follow Me. Their physical eyes cannot see Me, but their spiritual eyes and the eyes of their hearts have a vision of Me that is moving and with power.

"This world is filled to the brim with sickness, immorality, isolation, greed, desolation, anger, and fear, yet when I outstretch My arms and people choose to come into them and enter into My rest, I begin to reverse these conditions of the enemy and restore the order of people's hearts and lives. For with the decision to let Me into the heart there first was demonstrated a hope, which led to a growing faith, which led and built up to an outpouring of love—the love of God, which no man can measure and which no man can truly imagine.

"One simple yet profound message to this world that Satan seeks to devour and destroy—and that message is Me. I am Jesus, Lord of all Creation, Helper, Deliverer, Overcomer, Redeemer! Servant! Here to serve and minister to those who say "Yes" to Me and who continue to say "Yes" as they give over more and more of their lives to Me. Their lives are not their own any longer. They belong to Me. Yet My care is infinitely tender, infinitely merciful, wholly complete, and completely transforming.

"My promises do not change—and I am faithful to My promises. Until that glorious day when we meet face to face in the mansion where I go to prepare a room for each of My children—abide with Me and remember My promises."

Hebrews 13:8
Jesus Christ is the same yesterday and today and forever.

Ephesians 3:16
I pray that out of his glorious riches he may strengthen you with power through his Spirit in your inner being, 17 so that Christ may dwell in your hearts through faith. And I pray that you, being rooted and established in love, 18 may have power, together with all the Lord's holy people, to grasp how wide and long and high and deep is the love of Christ, 19 and to know this love that surpasses knowledge—that you may be filled to the measure of all the fullness of God.

REVIVAL!

"Pray for revival! Pray for My children to empty out their souls to Me, to repent of all their poor choices and continual sin.

"Even as I forgive their sin, they are brought closer to Me when there is the desire to go and sin no more, when there is a desire to please Me and live My way. And part of this is genuine repentance. Only with genuine repentance can revival occur. Repentance brings us closer together. Our relationship becomes fresher, cleaner, and holier."

"Get ready for a harvest of souls! Pray in My name—Jesus!—to bring them in, as I draw them to Me and convict them. Pray in My name—Jesus!—for My deliverance, and for My fire and glory to sweep this land in an unparalleled move of My Holy Spirit. Turn your faces towards Me and lift your arms high in praise and worship to Me, the one true God. Pray in My name—Jesus!—that I will equip you with all that you need and with all that is necessary in order for you to be actively part of revival. Pray in My name—Jesus!—without ceasing! For you are My body, the body of Christ, serving and loving each other and Me, your mighty and merciful and redeeming precious Savior.

"In My name, the mighty name of Jesus! Hallelujah!!!

> *Psalm 40:3*
> *He put a new song in my mouth,*
> *a hymn of praise to our God.*
> *Many will see and fear the Lord*
> *and put their trust in him.*

Joel 2:12

"Even now," declares the LORD, "return to me with all your heart, with fasting and weeping and mourning." 13 Rend your heart and not your garments. Return to the LORD your God, for he is gracious and compassionate, slow to anger and abounding in love, and he relents from sending calamity.

SEEKING AND SERVING JESUS

"Pouring perfume over Me was a most precious act of service given to Me. So it is as I require from all My children—that they give their best of service to Me, to each other, and to their world. That they faithfully seek and serve Me first, and the outpouring and overflowing of that is their desire to serve and care for and love each other. The very best acts of service come from an unselfish heart, a heart stripped bare of its idolatry and deceit, a heart cleansed with repentance of sin, a heart that is softened, turned, and yielded to Me.

"Putting others before yourself is only truly possible when you put Me first, when I am in the center of your life. And be not boastful of what you do for others, remember to be secret about it and humble, gentle and not self-seeking the glory. For the glory is Mine. What is yours is a promise of an unending grace and an undying love for all Eternity, freed from the shackles of the chains the enemy seeks to bind you with.

"So go in peace, My dearest, most treasured child, filled with the desire to serve, care for, and love others as I have loved you. Go in peace, secure in the knowledge that you are sanctified and secure within the mind and the body of Christ and promised to Me for Eternity."

> *Matthew 6:1*
> *"Be careful not to practice your righteousness in front of others to be seen by them. If you do, you will have no reward from your Father in heaven."*

> *Mark 14:3*
> *While he was in Bethany, reclining at the table in the home of Simon the Leper, a woman came with an alabaster jar of very expensive perfume, made of pure nard. She broke the jar and poured the perfume on his head.*

4 Some of those present were saying indignantly to one another, "Why this waste of perfume? 5 It could have been sold for more than a year's wages and the money given to the poor." And they rebuked her harshly. 6 "Leave her alone," said Jesus. "Why are you bothering her? She has done a beautiful thing to me. 7 The poor you will always have with you, and you can help them any time you want. But you will not always have me. 8 She did what she could. She poured perfume on my body beforehand to prepare for my burial. 9 Truly I tell you, wherever the gospel is preached throughout the world, what she has done will also be told, in memory of her."

THE LEAST BECOMES
THE GREATEST

"I created you and then I waited for you. Waited for you to come to Me. Yet I was always there with you. You never walked alone.

"Decide each day to renew your relationship with Me, My dearest, most precious child. For I seek this relationship with you above all else, to be close and supportive with you, to journey with you.

"Through prayer, listening for My voice, reading My Holy Scripture, through fasting, and in our own times of special communication through tongues, I am seeking to spend time with you. I look for you each day. That is why I am your Savior and you are My precious child. I want to be with you. You are My creation. I love you dearly and unreservedly. Obey and trust what I have for you and My instructions to you.

"Follow My voice only. For the enemy in his lying deceit can attempt to speak into you with his voice. Do not be fooled. As you wear your armor that comes through immersing yourself in the things of Me, his ability to deceive becomes less and less. His attempts may become more frequent as he seeks to attack and wound—yet I say to you that his ability to do so becomes less.

"Remember he has already been defeated. Do not be fooled by his ways to distract and bring you unease. And remember always that from the moment you gave your heart to Me you became Mine. You became Mine. You are always Mine now. So be with Me now."

Psalm 72:11
May all kings bow down to him
and all nations serve him.

Isaiah 9:6
For to us a child is born, to us a son is given, and the government will be
on his shoulders. And he will be called Wonderful Counselor, Mighty God,
Everlasting Father, Prince of Peace.

ALTARS IN HIGH PLACES

"The road to My truth is narrow and rocky. Your pathway through it needs to be kept straight and true. Do not deviate from My teachings. There is danger in the time that you live in, with many influences all purporting to be the way to go, many doctrines being preached, many religions and mishmash of religions being practiced. There are altars in high places out of your sight which need to be brought down and destroyed.

"Where are the altars in high places of *your* life? Those parts of you where you worship other gods before Me—the god of idolatry in particular. What do you worship besides Me? Shopping, TV stars, social media, games of chance, alcohol, drugs, false religions, busyness, food? What characteristics are marring your walk with Me—greed, envy, jealousy, judgment, hardheartedness, stubbornness? There are so many more. I want you to seek these altars out and commit to tearing them down. They do not serve you. They hinder your walk with Me.

"Just as a garden requires weeding and pruning, planting and sowing, so too do you need to be constantly and repeatedly vigilant about what influences you allow into your mind and what lifestyle you choose to lead. Weed out any ungodly or destructive influences and lifestyle choices. If left unchecked, they will eventually take over and strangle what has grown within you. Allow Me to prune those parts of your life which require new input. Plant and sow the seeds of righteous behavior according to what I have instructed in My Scriptures.

"My way is narrow and requires constant and careful vigilance, yet it results in expansion and the building of your character. It results in the deepening of your relationship with Me and the broadening of what I require. You are My disciple and My child and I require nothing less than total obedience to Me.

"Keep watch over all aspects of your life in accordance to the principles I have laid down in My Holy Scriptures. Stay true to My word and to Me. Remember what your inheritance is. Carry out your daily tasks with joy and expectancy, knowing all has been done already and taken care of. Peace be with you, beloved child. Peace be with you."

> *2 Kings 14:3*
> *He did what was right in the eyes of the Lord, but not as his father David had done. In everything he followed the example of his father Joash. 4 The high places, however, were not removed; the people continued to offer sacrifices and burn incense there.*

> *1 Corinthians 10:19*
> *Do I mean then that food sacrificed to an idol is anything, or that an idol is anything? 20 No, but the sacrifices of pagans are offered to demons, not to God, and I do not want you to be participants with demons. 21 You cannot drink the cup of the Lord and the cup of demons too; you cannot have a part in both the Lord's table and the table of demons. 22 Are we trying to arouse the Lord's jealousy? Are we stronger than he?*

REFLECTION:
THE LIGHT OF THE WORLD

The light is pouring down on me and it is coming from Jesus, the light of the world. He is illumination personified, the pure stream of living water infused with the light of God's glory and radiance. His light is healing, it is truth, it is love, it is mercy, it is forgiveness, it is purity. The light of the world is a balm to my wounds and a promise for freedom that is priceless beyond measure.

Eternally He promises to journey with us; eternally He will be waiting for us at the end of our lives. He is the prize at the end of the race. Yet the prize has already been given to us the day He chooses us. He reaches down and scoops us up in the loving embrace of His forgiveness. His goodness and glory are unable to be measured.

His intent is for rich relationship with us. He wants to spend time with us; He yearns for us. Let us also yearn for Lord Jesus with every fiber of our being. Let us lose ourselves in the truth and the teaching and the mystery of His ways. We lose ourselves in Him and find a Creator who is dazzling in His purity and mighty in His blessed plan for our goodness and His glory.

We are more than conquerors in our Lord Jesus; we surrender to Him and find victory in all that He offers us. So come, our precious, mighty, trustworthy, faithful Jesus—come! Name above all names. We praise You and we thank You for all that You are, all that You have done. We praise You and we thank You for giving us a hope and a future and a promise that we will never walk alone again.

Our Redeemer lives!

Job 19:25

I know that my redeemer lives, and that in the end he will stand on the earth. 26 And after my skin has been destroyed, yet in my flesh I will see God; 27 I myself will see him with my own eyes—I, and not another. How my heart yearns within me!

Jude 20

But you, dear friends, by building yourselves up in your most holy faith and praying in the Holy Spirit, 21 keep yourselves in God's love as you wait for the mercy of our Lord Jesus Christ to bring you to eternal life.

SECTION 11

CULTIVATE A HEART
OF THANKFULNESS

"Cultivate a heart of thankfulness. For there is thankfulness to be had and thankfulness to be given for every opportunity and circumstance of life.

"Be thankful for the clothes you wear, the food you eat, the car you drive, the people in your life—not just your family and friends but all those you know, all those you meet, all those you see in passing.

"Be thankful for the surroundings of nature, the trees, the sky, the sun, the flowers, for even the tiniest blade of grass underneath your feet.

"Be thankful for the miracle creation of the intricacies of your body, all of your senses within it, the way it functions so perfectly and beautifully, the breath in your lungs.

"Be thankful for the One who gave you breath!!! Praise and worship Me, adore Me at every opportunity!!!

"And be thankful also for the hardships of your life; the circumstances that cause you grief and distress.

"Be thankful for the way this lost and hurting world appears to be under the dominion of the enemy and spiraling ever downward—pray at every opportunity for the lost and hurting souls to turn to Me! Though it be difficult, painful, and challenging for you, be thankful for this apparent downward spiral, for it shows you that the time is closer, the time is coming ever nearer, to when I shall return in all of My glory for you and all My children, all those who love Me.

"Be thankful you still have even one more minute of breath in your body because this is an indicator your journey is not finished and your race is not run. You still have time and opportunity to share the gospel with those who are unreached. Remember I can give you the words and the way in which to share this. Be thankful that you are a sanctified child of God under My Holy and redeeming grace and you will be with Me forever, in Eternity.

"So, My dearest and most precious child, cultivate thankfulness within your heart. For this thankfulness and gratitude for what I have given you and for who you are in Me will see you stride through the circumstances of your life, emboldened, unafraid, enriched, and untouched by the enemy's attempts to stifle My work through you.

"I love you truly and forevermore. Go now and share My gospel—share My good news! Help bring that harvest in!"

> *Psalm 30:12*
> *that my heart may sing your praises and not be silent.*
> *LORD my God, I will praise you forever.*

> *1 Thessalonians 5:16*
> *Rejoice always, 17 pray continually, 18 give thanks in all circumstances;*
> *for this is God's will for you in Christ Jesus.*

HOLY SPIRIT FIRE!

"Fire! The fire of My Holy Spirit burning through you and setting you ablaze for Me! Purifying, sanctifying, edifying. Just like the three survived the fire, so too shall you, in your deepest tests and trials, survive with Me by your side. Being courageous and bold, stepping outside your comfort zone, and giving all to God humbly and without question. This is what I require of you.

"I am with you—with a might of radical, unsurpassed power. I give you courage whenever you require—yet you must ask for this. I ask you to serve Me, the one true God, no matter the cost and no matter how a situation appears. Know I am with you; know that My Holy Spirit is sent to be with you to guide you in My ways.

"As the fire of God's word is a purifying fire, allow it to purify and transform you from the inside out, beginning with your precious heart. Let the love of God become a raging furnace within your heart. Let this purifying, radiant fire open your spiritual eyes to see as I want you to see and to listen and discern the voice of God as you follow the instructions given in Holy Scripture.

"You can be assured of victory through Me when you trust and obey and give willingly that which I require—all of you. Total surrender to Me, to My Holy will, living by faith and not by sight, remembering that I have a Plan for your life, remembering My promises and My goodness, mercy, and sweet redemptive grace. I will not send you where I have not been. I will not send you where I am not.

"Step into the fire when it is required and allow Me to purify you and to burn away all that no longer serves you as a child of the Most High and One True God. Take courage, knowing I am with you. Allow yourself to

157

be consumed by the God of Miracles and Wonder, who loves you more than you can possibly imagine, who gave the life of His only son for your salvation, so that you could live together in Paradise with Him forevermore."

> *Daniel 3:23*
> *and these three men, firmly tied, fell into the*
> *blazing furnace. 24 Then King Nebuchadnezzar leaped*
> *to his feet in amazement and asked his advisers, "Weren't*
> *there three men that we tied up and threw into the fire?"*
> *They replied, "Certainly, Your Majesty." 25 He said,*
> *"Look! I see four men walking around in the fire, unbound and unharmed,*
> *and the fourth looks like a son of the gods."*

TINY DETAILS,
BIGGER BLESSINGS

"I made each and every one of the stars. Each and every one of them was crafted perfectly and uniquely by Me. I know all about them. They are the light shining in a dark night sky, something of beauty, of serenity and peace. As am I. Looking at the stars gives you a sense that there is order throughout the Universe. There is vastness throughout the Universe such that you cannot count the number of stars there are.

"Yet I as their Creator—and the Creator of yourself and all else that exists—know exactly how many stars there are. I know all about them. I know exactly how many grains of sand there are. I know all about them. I know exactly how many hairs there are on your head. I know all about you. I know all about these tiny details of life. And that is one of the places where I can be found. Within these tiny details.

"So look for Me there. Seek Me and acknowledge Me within the very tiny things that happen within your life. And as you make a habit of and grow accustomed to seeking Me in the smaller things, so shall your faith grow and you then begin to see Me in the bigger things.

"Continue to do this and your relationship of faith with Me will also continue to deepen, broaden, and open out. You will start to see the bigger picture and the way in which all things in this world connect together as part of that one bigger picture, that glorious bigger picture of and for and about Me. And as you seek Me in the tiny, fine details of life and give thanks for My presence there, you grow in your ability to handle the bigger details in My name.

"Praying and giving thanks for these tiny details and blessings in your life opens the door for bigger and wider blessings to come in. Give with a heart full of Me, give of yourself in all ways that I have ordained and authorized through My Holy Scripture. Give it all to Me prayerfully and joyously, knowing that I am the Source—all comes from Me.

"You belong to Me now and forevermore, My precious and redeemed child of God."

Job 26:7
He spreads out the northern skies over empty space; he suspends the earth over nothing. 8 He wraps up the waters in his clouds, yet the clouds do not burst under their weight. 9 He covers the face of the full moon, spreading his clouds over it. 10 He marks out the horizon on the face of the waters for a boundary between light and darkness. 11 The pillars of the heavens quake, aghast at his rebuke. 12 By his power he churned up the sea; by his wisdom he cut Rahab to pieces. 13 By his breath the skies became fair; his hand pierced the gliding serpent. 14 And these are but the outer fringe of his works; how faint the whisper we hear of him! Who then can understand the thunder of his power?

Philippians 4:19
And my God will meet all your needs according to the riches of his glory in Christ Jesus.

SPIRIT-FILLED, SANCTIFIED AND HOLY

"What would you give up to be closer to Me? If I asked you, what would you sacrifice?

"For what I have asked, as shown throughout My Holy Scriptures of those such as Esther, Ruth, Naomi, David, Daniel, Gideon, Jonah, Joshua, Joseph, Noah, Moses, Elijah, Paul—to name a few—is a requirement of total obedience lived out in total faith in Me. These beautiful, perfectly imperfect, broken children of Mine did as I required, trembling in fear and filled with doubt as they stepped out truly in faith and trust and followed Me. For I was always with them. And I am always with you.

"The enemy has also asked of Me, and I have given permission in the cases of people such as My faithful servant Job and My disciple Peter, to be challenged in their faith in Me. Know this—all that I ask has been and is in accordance with My Holy will, under My Holy grace, for My glory and for the good of the child of God involved. And so it is with you, precious one.

"And I do not ask anything of you that My Father and I would not and have not willingly given Ourselves. For My Father who art in Heaven willingly gave My life—the life of His only begotten son—to die a lowly, excruciatingly painful death, taking on the crushing burden of past, present, and future sin, so that the relationship between you and I could be restored and so that we could be together for all Eternity.

"Ask for Me to cultivate obedience and willingness to obey within you, My precious child. Keep that lifeline between us secure through prayer, fasting, reading My Scriptures, listening for My voice, being with other believers, praising and worshiping Me. Make every second of your existence a constant communion between the two of us.

"I require all of you, for you to die to yourself, so that I can be your first priority and you can live a Christ-centered existence, spirit-filled, sanctified and holy. The more you seek relationship with Me, the more you allow Me to enrich and uplift you, and to expand your heart and mind to accommodate your growing faith.

"Do not concern yourself with what My requirements may appear to be through your fleshly eyes. Look to My requirements using your spiritual eyes. Step out in faith boldly, knowing I have a plan to expand your life for My glory and your ultimate good."

> *Luke 8:10*
> *He said, "The knowledge of the secrets of the kingdom of God has been given to you, but to others I speak in parables, so that, "'though seeing, they may not see; though hearing, they may not understand.'*

> *Luke 22:31*
> *"Simon, Simon, Satan has asked to sift all of you as wheat. But I have prayed for you, Simon, that your faith may not fail. And when you have turned back, strengthen your brothers."*

NEVER ALONE

"Desolation, isolation, despair, depression, desperation, sorrow so deep it feels as though you will die from the weight of it, bone-breaking, aching loneliness—all of these are part of the human condition and a consequence of the fallen world. These are designed by the enemy to trap and trick the sufferer into believing that they are alone.

"The truth is, not one part of My creation—from the tiniest speck of dust to the vast expanse of the Universe; and especially My masterpiece, man—was designed to exist in isolation. All life and expressions of life are inter-connected and exist as parts of a greater whole.

"The lie of the enemy is designed to alienate man from not only each other and the world that they live in, but also from Me, their Creator. Yet the truth is that I am, and always have been, here—present, constant, faithful, and enduring; the author of your faith and the Creator of you and your world. I have created each man or woman with an expanse within that only I as their Creator can fill and satisfy. This is part of your design.

"So there is a yearning that can only be filled by Me. This yearning can be filled momentarily from without by the distractions of the fallen world or filled a little longer from within by relationships with each other. Yet it is only I, your God, who can fully and permanently fill both within and without—with Me, with My majesty, My glory, and My unparalleled might! Yet I also created each man with free will and each has a choice as to whether or not their free will is exercised to accept Me.

"Your part as a believer and overcomer in Me is to pray unceasingly for those who are desolate, isolated, despairing, depressed, desperate, sorrowful, lonely, and cut off from Me. Pray that there will be a seeking for Me. Pray that each precious lost and hurting soul will find Me and drink from the sweetness of My living water; that each precious lost and hurting soul will accept Me; that each precious lost and hurting soul will find salvation and transformation in the arms of the God who loves them with a fierce depth and jealousy that no force of darkness can stand against.

"And be ready to have your prayers answered; be ready to be put in the pathway of those who are seeking; be ready to fulfil your part in My Great Commission, sharing your faith and the Holy power of the gospel through the power of My Holy Spirit that instructs and guides you.

"I am with you to the end of the age."

> *Deuteronomy 11:1*
> *Love the LORD your God and keep his requirements, his decrees, his laws and his commands always.*

> *John 4:13*
> *Jesus answered, "Everyone who drinks this water will be thirsty again, but whoever drinks the water I give them will never thirst. Indeed, the water I give them will become in them a spring of water welling up to eternal life."*

COMMUNION

"Just as this bread is broken into pieces, so too remember My body broken for you on the Cross. And just as this wine is poured out, so too remember My precious blood poured out for you. My body and My blood offered as the sacrifice and atonement for all the sin that has ever, or will ever, exist in those who choose to believe in Me.

"I am alive now, My precious child, I no longer hang on that Cross. Yet it is a powerful symbol of redemption and you are able to partake in that power by bringing worries, memories, and all else that makes your spirit restless straight to the foot of My Holy Cross. My blood can pour out over these and wash them clean, transforming them in My name, the name above all names.

"As we eat this bread together, remember also that I am the bread of your life. I want you to realize that you have a hunger that is spiritual and not just one that is physical. The spiritual hunger is a yearning for Me, and I want you to get used to the idea that you need to also experience physical hunger at times as a sacrifice to Me. These are the mandatory times of fasting. The words given in My Holy Scriptures are "when you fast," and it is important to come close to Me in this way and realize that My Holy Word and time with Me is what is needed to truly satisfy your hunger.

"The development of self-control is one of the fruits of the Spirit, child of God, and your body is to be made a Holy and acceptable sacrifice to Me. So that your prayer life may be focused with intensity, fasting is necessary. Allow Me to fill your body and quell those hunger pangs through My Holy Spirit and the living, breathing words of My Holy Scriptures.

"Let these times of communion with Me refresh and revitalize your parched spirit, and bring you back into the sweetness of My unending grace and mercy. All is made plain and simple within My overcoming forgiveness."

Matthew 4:4

Jesus answered, "It is written: 'Man shall not live on bread alone, but on every word that comes from the mouth of God.'"

1 Corinthians 11:23

For I received from the Lord what I also passed on to you: The Lord Jesus, on the night he was betrayed, took bread, 24 and when he had given thanks, he broke it and said, "This is my body, which is for you; do this in remembrance of me." 25 In the same way, after supper he took the cup, saying, "This cup is the new covenant in my blood; do this, whenever you drink it, in remembrance of me." 26 For whenever you eat this bread and drink this cup, you proclaim the Lord's death until he comes.

REFLECTION:
HIS EVERLASTING
CARE AND LOVE

Jesus looked for me—His one little sheep that strayed from the flock. He came in search of me, His one lost little sheep. All who do not know our Lord Jesus Christ are like lost little sheep that He goes after, desiring all to come to salvation.

And what He offers is like the most perfect fathering/mothering of all; nothing can harm us when we are in the embrace and tender care of our Lord Jesus. Nothing can come between Him and us. He is everlasting in His care and love for us. He is completely transfixed by us, His creations. His love is a love that is pure and perfect; it is a love that disciplines, guides, soothes, heals, protects, cares for, and endures into Eternity.

So I stay in the warm and soothing embrace of my Lord Jesus Christ. He is faithful, and oh, so trustworthy! I can give all that pains me straight to Him; I can take it straight to the foot of His Holy Cross; and He can take it and transform it. He keeps on refining me, healing me, reshaping and reworking my heart into a heart of flesh and softness; a heart of power and purity.

All for Him. I realize it is all for Him. Jesus is Lord—pure and unsurpassable Majesty, yet able to soothe my troubled spirit with just one moment of being in His awesome Presence. He is close to us every second of our existence—for when we come to Him, we truly do come to Him, we abide in Him, and we become part of His body, the body of Christ.

We work out our salvation in fear and trembling because of the awesome power of our Savior and King; yet we are also uplifted and soothed most perfectly by His unending and perfect love, drenched in the power of His forgiveness and saturated with the might of His glory and grace.

Hallelujah! We are free!

> *Philippians 4:4*
> *Rejoice in the Lord always. I will say it again: Rejoice! 5 Let your gentleness be evident to all. The Lord is near. 6 Do not be anxious about anything, but in every situation, by prayer and petition, with thanksgiving, present your requests to God. 7 And the peace of God, which transcends all understanding, will guard your hearts and your minds in Christ Jesus.*

> *James 4:8*
> *Come near to God and he will come near to you. Wash your hands, you sinners, and purify your hearts, you double-minded. Grieve, mourn and wail. Change your laughter to mourning and your joy to gloom. Humble yourselves before the Lord, and he will lift you up.*

SECTION 12

I AM YOUR SAVIOR

"I am your Savior—faithful and loving, constant and reassuring.

"I am your Savior—My unmatched strength spoke all of Creation into existence, yet I am able to tenderly hold your weak spirit and raw, fragile heart safely in My hands.

"I am your Savior—I willingly laid down My life for you so that I could have a relationship with you.

"I am your Savior—I give you rest and rejuvenation and I cultivate a richness of relationship you could never have imagined was possible.

"I promise you My unending love, mercy, goodness, and grace, flowing over you and filling each moment within your day, humbling you, uplifting you, bringing joy and comfort as you grow in Me.

"I am here, quiet, allowing you to be and rest in Me, the Lord of your soul!"

Psalm 86:15
But you, Lord, are a compassionate and gracious God,
slow to anger, abounding in love and faithfulness.

John 3:16
For God so loved the world that he gave his one and only Son, that whoever believes in him shall not perish but have eternal life. 17 For God did not send his Son into the world to condemn the world, but to save the world through him.

ON MARRIAGE

"I am to be made the center and the first priority in any marriage. It is easier said than done. Yet it is also profoundly simple. Be willing to obey My instructions for the marriage and stay close to Me in each moment within the marriage. I am the pivotal point for success in any marriage, and for true and godly growth of both the marriage and the participants within it.

"A marriage where both husband and wife serve and love and care for each other according to My principles and with their focus on Me is indeed a marriage made in Heaven. The potential for a battleground to develop is always present and is what the enemy desires more than anything else. The healing of wounds in safety and security, with love, is what is needed in a marriage. A godly couple with their eyes fixed on Me can accomplish this.

"I can bring a couple together but I will not tear them apart. Only the couple involved can do this. There can be a tearing apart and irreparable damage, especially through violence and unfaithfulness, and the marriage covenant is shattered.

"So to build or rebuild a marriage on My principles—asking and praying fervently for My help, giving thanks to Me for the blessing of the marriage, with clearly defined ways in which husband and wife are to serve each other within the marriage, focused on Me and then each other with laser-sharp intensity—is to build a marriage that is strong and true and rock solid. The journey of marriage is perhaps the most difficult yet also the most enriching of all journeys.

"One man and one woman come together with the desire to love and be of service to one another, with friendship and encouragement for one another, yoked equally together in a blessed union. This is marriage. Good, growing, godly marriage."

Genesis 2:20

So the man gave names to all the livestock, the birds in the sky and all the wild animals. But for Adam no suitable helper was found. 21 So the Lord God caused the man to fall into a deep sleep; and while he was sleeping, he took one of the man's ribs and then closed up the place with flesh. 22 Then the Lord God made a woman from the rib he had taken out of the man, and he brought her to the man. 23 The man said, "This is now bone of my bones and flesh of my flesh; she shall be called 'woman,' for she was taken out of man." 24 That is why a man leaves his father and mother and is united to his wife, and they become one flesh.

Ephesians 5:22

Wives, submit yourselves to your own husbands as you do to the Lord. 23 For the husband is the head of the wife as Christ is the head of the church, his body, of which he is the Savior. 24 Now as the church submits to Christ, so also wives should submit to their husbands in everything. 25 Husbands, love your wives, just as Christ loved the church and gave himself up for her 26 to make her holy, cleansing her by the washing with water through the word.

FOLLOWING JESUS

"Following Me is profoundly simple—give your life to Me. Take up your Cross. Trust Me with every aspect of your life. It goes against your fallen nature and brokenness to trust Me, to give over control of your life to Me.

"Yet I say to you, this is the key to entering into truest relationship with me. This allows for an unparalleled richness of relationship to develop and grow between the two of us. For My plan for your life is huge and magnificent, intricate and beyond anything you could imagine. Yet your part in this plan is simple—let go of your own desires and designs on your life and follow Me.

"Keep your eyes on Me, My precious child. Seek Me and rest in Me earnestly in every waking moment that you have. Communicate with Me through prayer, supplication, thanksgiving, praise, and worship in every waking moment that you have. Remember to be in this world but not of it—conform not to its ways but commit to My ways; you are passing through it on the way to Eternity. Glorify Me through the sacrifice of your life to Me, knowing that I have already made the ultimate sacrifice to free you and enter into right relationship with you. Grace has paid your debt in full. It is of no consequence that this is not something you deserve—the gift of salvation is freely given to those who accept and turn to Me. Right relationship with you is what I as your Creator yearns for.

"Step into the full potential of what I have waiting for you, My beautiful, broken, dearest child of God. You do not need to know where each of our footsteps together will take you—only trust Me and rest securely in the knowledge that our journey is leading to where I want you to be. I am building you strong and true from the inside out, guiding you with My sure and steady instructions, growing you straight and true like a towering oak tree. And this journey will continue until the day I call you Home.

"Make each moment count. Do not waste an instant being distracted from your purpose of glorifying Me in whatever you do in the moments that make up your life. For you will not pass this way again."

Psalm 40:5
Many, LORD my God,
are the wonders you have done,
the things you planned for us.
None can compare with you;
were I to speak and tell of your deeds,
they would be too many to declare.

Romans 5:15
But the gift is not like the trespass. For if the many died by the trespass of the one man, how much more did God's grace and the gift that came by the grace of the one man, Jesus Christ, overflow to the many! 16 Nor can the gift of God be compared with the result of one man's sin: The judgment followed one sin and brought condemnation, but the gift followed many trespasses and brought justification.

LETTING GO INTO JESUS

"Times where you come before Me and simply meditate on My presence and be with Me are vital for the deepening of our relationship.

"Think of Me and let My love for you wash over you and through you, filling you up and strengthening you.

"Think of Me and let My will for you reveal itself.

"Think about Me speaking the whole world and all the universes into creation.

"Think of Me being born in a stable to a teenage girl and what this would have been like for her.

"Think of Me in any situation of your life which needs guidance. And let My guidance come gently for you. Let My guidance come through for you. For all has been done for you already at Calvary.

"My precious child, our relationship is one of 'let go.' Only hang on when it is to Me. Letting go means surrendering. And instantly, at that moment of surrender, there is a relief. The burdens slip away. The tension leaves. And that precise moment is when I step in and take the burdens for you, dissolving the tension and replacing it with acceptance—acceptance that I am able, that I am willing, that I am here just for you, that I am faithful, that I am constant, that I am merciful. That I Am. I strengthen you and allow you to continue on.

"So release your burdens unto Me.

"Walk with Me."

HEARING HIS VOICE

Proverbs 2:6
For the LORD gives wisdom;
from his mouth come knowledge and understanding.
7 He holds success in store for the upright,
he is a shield to those whose walk is blameless,
8 for he guards the course of the just
and protects the way of his faithful ones.
9 Then you will understand what is right and just
and fair—every good path.

Hosea 2:19
I will betroth you to me forever; I will betroth you in righteousness and
justice, in love and compassion. 20 I will betroth you in faithfulness, and
you will acknowledge the Lord.

FLY? OR NOT?

"When the baby bird is ready to fly, its mother brings it to the edge of the nest and pushes it out. It has no choice but to fly.

"And so it is with you, My precious one, My beautiful broken child of God. I bring you to the edge of yourself and you have that same choice. Fly? Or not? This is essentially the edge of your comfort zone. And I am there. Yet I am also within your comfort zone.

"Within and without, I am your comforter and strengthener. I am with you. I guide and oversee all of the footsteps of your journey, dearest child, and you can be assured that all is in order within that journey. It may not seem that way to you at times, yet I say to you that this is the truth of our walk together.

"I transform you from the inside out and this requires challenging you. But fear not. You are an overcomer within Me.

"So step out boldly in faith and move outside of your comfort zone when and where it is required, knowing that I am with you.

"Abide with me."

> *John 15:7*
> *If you remain in me and my words remain in you, ask whatever you wish, and it will be done for you. 8 This is to my Father's glory, that you bear much fruit, showing yourselves to be my disciples. 9 "As the Father has loved me, so have I loved you. Now remain in my love. 10 If you keep my commands, you will remain in my love, just as I have kept my Father's*

commands and remain in his love. 11 I have told you this so that my joy may be in you and that your joy may be complete. 12 My command is this: Love each other as I have loved you.

1 Corinthians 16:13
Be on your guard; stand firm in the faith; be courageous; be strong. 14 Do everything in love.

SUSTAINING FAITH

"There will be times of intense darkness within your life, dearest one. Times where your faith is challenged relentlessly, and times where you may even feel abandoned by Me. Times where you only have small sparks of lightness here and there amidst circumstances of seemingly unfixable turmoil.

"Yet know without doubt that I am with you and that what you are experiencing are times of intense growth also. If you are able to sustain your faith in Me and not be swayed by outer circumstances, you will find that your perseverance develops and in turn your character builds and is strengthened in hope—My hope. Let your faith in Me be solid as a rock, an anchor keeping you close to Me. All that you need is available for you within Me and My promises.

"There is nothing you need to do differently when circumstances are beneficial or when circumstances are difficult. In all circumstances turn to Me, yield to Me, keep your eyes fixed on Me. In all cases I will be the light within your darkness. In all cases give thanks and praise and worship and you will be purified through the fire of your suffering to glorify Me.

"Practice doing this, My child—practice not being attached to what seems to be this way or that way in the physical world that you walk in. Only practice being attached to Me and allow Me to complete the work I have begun in you.

"For this is true growth. You will know this if you give all to Me and allow Me to walk with you and bring you safely forward. Know this. Be with Me."

Romans 5:1

Therefore, since we have been justified through faith, we have peace with God through our Lord Jesus Christ, 2 through whom we have gained access by faith into this grace in which we now stand. And we boast in the hope of the glory of God. 3 Not only so, but we also glory in our sufferings, because we know that suffering produces perseverance; 4 perseverance, character; and character, hope. 5 And hope does not put us to shame, because God's love has been poured out into our hearts through the Holy Spirit, who has been given to us. 6 You see, at just the right time, when we were still powerless, Christ died for the ungodly.

REFLECTION:
PERFECT HARMONY

"The order of God's world! Nothing chaotic. Everything in its place. An organized system running smoothly. Until the selfishness of sin seeped in. The ripple effect is still felt from that far-off day. Sin runs rampant in this fallen world of today. Yet how would it be if Adam and Eve had never eaten of the fruit of the Tree of Knowledge? Can you imagine living in perfect harmony with God? Can you imagine fellowshipping with God and He is real and present, a person in His form yet at the same time being the Creator of the Universe? Well, that is who Jesus was . . . and is.

God came to earth in the form of a man, in the form of His Son. And He allowed Himself to be nailed to a Cross. The fullness of deity, and He allowed Himself to take on sin that stretched above, behind, and in front of Him. He took on that sin to activate forgiveness and forge a relationship with mankind that set everything right again, that took us back to that junction point of the Tree of Knowledge. Only this time we make the perfect and right and true choice when we choose Jesus.

We are not at the Tree of Knowledge any longer, we are now at a tree that is a Cross, and we choose differently this time. We choose for our perfect Jesus. We choose knowing that our choice is the most powerful choice for good this time. We choose Jesus not because we have knowledge but because we lack salvation. We lack the promise of forgiveness, of redemption, of relationship with our Creator.

We can have all the knowledge available to us, the entire history of the world's knowledge and an intellect that is razor sharp, yet still not choose Jesus. What we gain with Jesus is far beyond knowledge and operates in the realm of faith. This is the power of trusting Him, sight unseen. This is the power of being saved by grace.

Then knowing Jesus, rather than just having knowledge of Him, starts to come in as we develop a personal relationship with Him. We live by faith, and the Holy Spirit breathed into us gives us the interpretation of Scripture and the desire to live for Jesus in obedience and trust. And this is an epic journey—and easier said than done!

How to be obedient to and how to trust our Savior with our lives is a journey unlike any other we will ever go on—a monumentally transforming journey where we are remade in Jesus' likeness. Where our hearts are transformed from a heart of stone into a heart of flesh. Where we give everything we are and everything we have to Jesus. Where we are willing to die to ourselves just as He died for us—so we can meet in relationship and spread the glory of His eternal lifesaving gospel.

Jesus, Lord Jesus, All in all, Deliverer, Conqueror, Redeemer, Perfect Savior, Creator, Good and Glorious Majesty! How we praise Your name. Our sins are forgiven; we are set free in the holy, redeeming, sweeter-than-sweet grace of Your tender mercy and love.

Who can comprehend our Savior's sacrifice? Who of us could ever possibly know what it meant to *become* sin? The mind of God is a mystery, yet we have the mind of Christ, His Holy Spirit, to guide us and light the way before us, to bring us out of the darkness and into the presence of the light of the world. Powerful, all-knowing, and pure love—Jesus. He sets us free, healing the deepest pain within us with His tender mercy.

There are no words adequate to express the gift of Jesus. We don't deserve Him now, we didn't deserve him 2,000 years ago—yet here He is, within us, for us always—because it is not about us, but it is all about

Him. His goodness! His grace. We praise Your name, Lord, and we thank You, thank You, thank You, for coming to us and saving us. Amazing grace!

> *Genesis 2:16*
> *And the LORD God commanded the man, "You are free to eat from any tree in the garden; but you must not eat from the tree of the knowledge of good and evil, for when you eat from it you will certainly die."*

> *Proverbs 1:7*
> *The fear of the LORD is the beginning of knowledge,*
> *but fools despise wisdom and instruction.*

SECTION 13

GIFTINGS

"You are part of the Great Commission. You have your part to play. Devotion to Me reveals this part to you. Cultivation of right relationship with and within Me makes this part crystal clear to you. Use your gifts wisely, dear and precious child. Use them for service to others and for My glorification.

"How do you know what your gifts are? Your gifts are those talents I have given you, the ways of your personality that bring you contentment and joy. They do not appear to be as work, but rather as something you are driven to do, something that is essential for your wellbeing, something that you enjoy and are able to do with ease and express yourself fully within.

"For some like yourself, your gifts are around writing, for others they are expressed through service, healing, hospitality, precision to detail, art, dramatic work—to name a few. Alongside your gifts are those parts of your personality which challenge you and which also need to be developed. These are more difficult to master. So if you have a personality trait of shyness, boldness is what you are required to develop. If you are prone to anger, then self-control is what you are required to develop. Joy would be the requirement as an antidote to being prone to depression.

"You are required to develop all of the fruit of the Spirit—so you seek out My guidance as to how this needs to occur. And as always when you ask Me, I will help you. Ask for all that you need in My name and it will be given to you in accordance to My will and the perfect plan I have for your life.

"And above all, My cherished and most beautiful creation, trust and have faith in Me—for I gave you life and then eternal life in Me, and I will bring you safely Home when the time is right and your race is run.

"I am with you always, My precious and beloved child of God."

> *1 Corinthians 12:4*
> *There are different kinds of gifts, but the same Spirit distributes them. 5 There are different kinds of service, but the same Lord. 6 There are different kinds of working, but in all of them and in everyone it is the same God at work. 7 Now to each one the manifestation of the Spirit is given for the common good.*

> *Romans 11:29*
> *For God's gifts and his call are irrevocable.*

HIS HOLY WORDS

"Each word of every book contained in My Bible is carefully measured and constructed to make a perfect whole. Each of these books are woven together to tell one story—of man's fall from perfect relationship with God, our Heavenly Father, and man's journey back into relationship with God, our Heavenly Father.

"I am the bridge spanning the two, the Old Testament and the New Testament, and I am the binding force that holds all the words together. I exist before Creation and I am the redeeming force of Creation, the One who came to set Creation free through My sacrifice at the Cross and My resurrection from the dead.

"Taken as a historical document, the Bible can be measured and verified for accuracy. But it is not the historical aspects that are of most importance, though there is undoubtedly a place for these. It is the relational aspects of the journey back into covenant under grace between God and His most treasured and cherished creation—mankind—which are of utmost importance. It is the story of those men and women of faith who God used mightily to glorify Himself.

"Their stories give encouragement and inspiration to the faith-filled reader. And when a believer becomes filled with the Holy Spirit and asks for the Holy Spirit to reveal the truths of Scripture, the Bible becomes a living and breathing masterpiece of God's ageless truth. The Holy Bible is the instruction manual for life and the Holy Spirit is the illuminating force which highlights and reveals these instructions.

"So, My dear child, know that My Holy Bible is vital in your walk with Me; its instructions for whatever is challenging in your life are priceless and ageless. Make sure to read and breathe in the truths that it conveys and ask the Holy Spirit to illuminate that which is most relevant for you at that particular time in your life. Let the men and women of faith become alive for you and realize that they faced so many of the same challenges you face right here and right now. They walked where you walk now. And just as I walked with them, I walk with you now.

"Continue to read your Bible as you walk with Me and allow My Holy Scriptures to guide your way moment by moment. Let your eyes read the words, let your ears hear what is being said, let your mind be filled with the truth of God and allow your heart—filled with the Holy Spirit—to discern what the message of each passage of Scripture is saying."

> *John 14:26*
> *But the Advocate, the Holy Spirit, whom the Father will send in my name, will teach you all things and will remind you of everything I have said to you. 27 Peace I leave with you; my peace I give you. I do not give to you as the world gives. Do not let your hearts be troubled and do not be afraid.*

> *2 Timothy 3:16*
> *All Scripture is God-breathed and is useful for teaching, rebuking, correcting and training in righteousness, 17 so that the servant of God may be thoroughly equipped for every good work.*

NOTHING WASTED

"I have come to serve you, to show you My way of and definition of love. Loving the Lord your God first and foremost and then loving one another as I have loved you. Loving your brothers, your sisters, your neighbors, your friends. Loving the imperfections of your fellow man, realizing that all are broken and all have fallen short.

"When I walked the earth, I was sinless and perfect, yet still I was crucified on that Cross of Calvary because that was how it had to be. It was My Father's will and My will also. My sacrifice on the Cross, with My body beaten, broken, and bloodied beyond recognition was at the same time love made visible, forgiveness poured out through My blood, sacrifice becoming grace, and the redemption of those who give themselves to Me. There was no other way.

"When I was tempted for 40 days in the wilderness there was no other way to begin My ministry. When I sweated blood in the garden at Gethsemane I knew there was no other way to prepare myself for the ordeal that was unfolding and would culminate in My death on the Cross. When I became God in human form there was no other way for a new covenant to be established. No other way.

"And so it is with you, My precious child, and the suffering that is a necessary part of your life—there is no other way. It cannot and must not be avoided. Every hardship you experience, every painful circumstance you live through, every time you weep tears of utter sorrow and desolation, every time you feel your heart could break for the complete devastation enveloping it—all of these are necessary in order to shape your character.

"Live in joy, free in the knowledge that I am with you always. There is nothing wasted within your life and the plan that defines your life— every circumstance is turned so that I am glorified and so that you can help others going through similar events and circumstances in their own lives. For compassion and empathy with others is a priceless treasure. To walk beside another human being, truly knowing what they are going through because you have walked a journey just like theirs is a gift that is beyond measure. To ease another's loneliness or isolation and to serve them by meeting them in their deepest need is a glorification of who I am and what I came to do.

"To love one another as I have loved you—with sacrifice and with selflessness, with care and compassion, free of condemnation and judgment—this is Christlike love made visible. So believe that I love you more deeply than you could ever imagine, My dearest child, and walk in this world fortified and strengthened by this love and for the forgiveness through grace that bonds us always. Our relationship is an eternal one, My precious child, forged in bonds of sacrificial love and bathed in the Holy blood of My forgiveness and redemption. I am with you always."

> *Luke 6:35*
> *But love your enemies, do good to them, and lend to them without expecting to get anything back. Then your reward will be great, and you will be children of the Most High, because he is kind to the ungrateful and wicked. 36 Be merciful, just as your Father is merciful. 37 Do not judge, and you will not be judged. Do not condemn, and you will not be condemned. Forgive, and you will be forgiven. 38 Give, and it will be given to you. A good measure, pressed down, shaken together and running over, will be poured into your lap. For with the measure you use, it will be measured to you."*

2 Corinthians 7:9

yet now I am happy, not because you were made sorry, but because your sorrow led you to repentance. For you became sorrowful as God intended and so were not harmed in any way by us. 10 Godly sorrow brings repentance that leads to salvation and leaves no regret, but worldly sorrow brings death.

TEMPTATION

"Temptation is everywhere in the natural world; so much a part of your everyday life, and even more so when you give your life to Me. You are required to resist temptation in so many ways! The pull of the natural world and of your fallen nature can at times appear to be very strong. Yet My pull is stronger. I am the antidote to the poison of temptation. As you journey with Me it will become easier to resist the temptation of the enemy. I have claimed you as My own; the enemy is merely trying to convince you of his lies and deception that masquerades as truth. His words are empty and without substance.

"To keep to My path of truth and adhere to My path of truth as laid out in the Scriptures is, at times, like walking a tightrope. The spirit is willing but the flesh is weak. The fallen fleshly nature seeks for you to collapse into addiction and other sinful behaviors, yet your spirit nature is always seeking to edify and uplift and serve those around you for My glory. Second by second is the choice of following Me and walking My path, glorifying Me—or believing the lies and indulging in those behaviors which distract, depress, and threaten to destroy who you are in Me.

"Keep your eyes on Me, precious child, and let My Holy Scriptures—illuminated by guidance from the Holy Spirit—a strong prayer life, being with other believers, and praise and worship, build the strongholds within you that allow you to resist and flee from the enemy's machinations.

"And when you do give into temptation and make those choices which do not reflect Me and My glory, then genuinely repent of these and commit to beginning again in Me. And My voice of grace, My covenant of undying forgiveness and love, will keep you safe within My flock.

You belong to Me! You belonged to Me from the moment you accepted Me into your heart, My precious child. And Satan hates you because of this!

"Yet he has already lost the battle for your eternal soul. So waste not one more minute with the worry and doubt that he delights in. They are empty and without substance. Walk with Me and rest assured that your God does not tempt you. Temptation is the hallmark of the enemy. Your God will test your faith and shape your character in accordance with His will and for your good. But He will never tempt you. Believe this and let this security grow strong and steady within you. I am with you. Rest in Me."

> *Hebrews 2:18*
> *Because he himself suffered when he was tempted, he is able to help those who are being tempted.*

> *2 Chronicles 20:15*
> *He said: "Listen, King Jehoshaphat and all who live in Judah and Jerusalem! This is what the LORD says to you: 'Do not be afraid or discouraged because of this vast army. For the battle is not yours, but God's.'*

HELLFIRE!

"Hell, eternal Hell and damnation, is very real, My child. It is a place of lethargy, of drudgery and hardship, misery and endless torment. It is the opposite of the Paradise that awaits every believer. And if you had a glimpse, just one glimpse, of the utter desolation that Hell entails, you would strive unceasingly to spread the hope of the message of My gospel.

We want none to be lost through not being given the message! It is one thing for a man to choose eternal damnation by hardening his heart against Me—it is another to never be given the message of hope; to never be given the opportunity to realize there is another way.

"I yearn for all to come to Me. Free will, however, gives each one the ability to choose, or not to choose, to come to Me. Yet if the reality of Hell could be shown as that which awaits the apathetic as well as the hardhearted, could be shown as that which awaits the unreached, then the choice may very well be made differently.

"I have overcome the world and it is My fervent desire for all those of the world to believe in Me. Yet I know that some will be lost. And My heart breaks for those. This is why it is every believer's responsibility to be busy scattering seed, as well as sowing and reaping. Spread the message of hope that is My Holy gospel and allow Me to take care of the seeds that you scatter, to bring them to fruition and ripeness in the hearts of those who are softened and ready to receive Me.

"You may never know the extent of your seed scattering while you are on Earth. Yet I say to you that when you reach your reward in Paradise you will see the fruits of your labors, glorifying Me. So go, do your very best to glorify Me and spread My message of the life-giving gospel through your words and your faith propelled works. Go now. Make haste. I am with you."

Matthew 9:38
Ask the Lord of the harvest, therefore, to send out workers into his harvest field."

Luke 8:11
"This is the meaning of the parable: The seed is the word of God. 12 Those along the path are the ones who hear, and then the devil comes and takes away the word from their hearts, so that they may not believe and be saved. 13 Those on the rocky ground are the ones who receive the word with joy when they hear it, but they have no root. They believe for a while, but in the time of testing they fall away. 14 The seed that fell among thorns stands for those who hear, but as they go on their way they are choked by life's worries, riches and pleasures, and they do not mature. 15 But the seed on good soil stands for those with a noble and good heart, who hear the word, retain it, and by persevering produce a crop.

LAY DOWN YOUR BURDEN

"Lay down your burden, My child, the burden where you believed you had to do everything, be everything, fill in the gaps, and work everything out. This has never been your job to do. This has always been Mine. You have pushed yourself to the point of exhaustion—and for what?

"My precious child, I gave you gifts and a heart to be used for My glory. Yet a stronghold from childhood and generations past has been implanted within you—to be overly responsible and dependent on your own strength to accomplish what I have always desired to accomplish *through* you, not *by* you. You have felt alone, so utterly alone, because of this over responsibility and seeking to do all yourself. There has been little room for Me. Pray in My Holy name for the stronghold to be crushed and all generational curses to be brought to My Holy Cross, to be washed clean and transformed. For I became a curse so that this could be so and so that you could be free.

"Now, precious child, child who belongs to Me, child of My heart— allow Me to be with you. You are realizing you are not alone—you are realizing you belong to Me and are therefore part of Me. We are together. I fill you with My Holy Spirit. I strengthen you with My protection. I fill your cup to overflowing with My blessings and thorough care. I lift you up with the power of My promises. I am faithful always. Only trust in Me—all of you, every part of you, every area of your life—physical, mental, emotional, spiritual—trust completely in Me.

"I can carry you through any storm. I can guide you through any storm. I can shelter you from any storm, I can be with you in any storm. Be with Me also—fully, completely, utterly, totally, and wholly—be with Me, My precious child.

"I love you with a fierce and jealous, unending and unyielding love. You are Mine and I am yours. My precious and cherished child. Know this."

1 John 4:12

No one has ever seen God; but if we love one another, God lives in us and his love is made complete in us. 13 This is how we know that we live in him and he in us: He has given us of his Spirit. 14 And we have seen and testify that the Father has sent his Son to be the Savior of the world. 15 If anyone acknowledges that Jesus is the Son of God, God lives in them and they in God. 16 And so we know and rely on the love God has for us. God is love. Whoever lives in love lives in God, and God in them. 17 This is how love is made complete among us so that we will have confidence on the day of judgment: In this world we are like Jesus. 18 There is no fear in love. But perfect love drives out fear, because fear has to do with punishment. The one who fears is not made perfect in love. 19 We love because he first loved us.

REFLECTION:
COPING ON MY OWN

I am laying a burden at My Lord Jesus' feet. This burden has been an unbearably heavy one and has weighed me down on more than one occasion. The burden is my pretense at coping; my false pride in my own strength; my willingness to believe that I can do it all, fix it all, work it all out. All on my own.

The truth is, I have never been able to cope on my own. I have had a good go at pretending otherwise, but I have come to realize I am not a one-man band. I realize that You, my precious Lord Jesus, are the only one who can do all for me. And that is not future tense. Because you have already done it all with Your sacrifice at the Cross. You have already bought my salvation with the purchase of my sin at the Cross.

So my yielding the burden to you is the recognition, in some small way, of the Might that is You. I want to die to self, to give all my thoughts to you. You can hold them captive in Your loving embrace. I belong to You and now I seek the will to do Your will, I seek to align myself with Your purpose for me, to bring You glory in every action, every thought, every word, every deed, every piece of my heart—every part of this journey of faith we are on.

I am not powerful; You are. I am not strong; You are. I am Your lost little sheep, Your tiny sinful child washed clean by the power of Your precious blood. Yet You, my mighty, majestic, most glorious, powerful, loving, forgiving Creator, have reached down and uplifted me to sit before Your throne of grace. All Your precious promises that speak of the joy of living a life for You, dear Lord Jesus, and of the inheritance of life eternal with You, are promises I believe to be true.

HEARING HIS VOICE

I catch glimpses of the unspeakable awesomeness of who You are and I pray that I am made worthy and presented to You as a good and faithful servant. Lord, keep my heart pure and spotless, that it may do Your bidding. Lord Jesus, help me to abide with You, eyes fixed on You, mouth worshiping You, Spirit praising You. For You are my all in all, Lord Jesus Christ. And Your yoke is easy and Your burden is light.

Glory Hallelujah!

John 3:30
He must become greater; I must become less.

2 Corinthians 1:3
Praise be to the God and Father of our Lord Jesus Christ, the Father of compassion and the God of all comfort, 4 who comforts us in all our troubles, so that we can comfort those in any trouble with the comfort we ourselves receive from God. 5 For just as we share abundantly in the sufferings of Christ, so also our comfort abounds through Christ.

SECTION 14

FAITH-FILLED JOURNEY

"Worshiping me, walking the way I direct, following My footsteps and staying in close communion and relationship with Me is the spirit life of a believer. A faith-filled journey is like a constant breathing in of the freshness and vibrancy of nature where all is vibrant, alive and growing, buoyant, changing with the seasons, yet constant.

"Just as each part of nature is different and unique, all parts combine together in harmony and order. This is like the body of believers, all different and unique, yet working together in harmony to praise, worship, trust, and obey Me. Each one a very integral and meaningful part, each one with a Holy Spirit breathed role to play, each one glorifying Me with action and word, and each one striving to run the very best race possible.

"And existing within this is the fleshly part of us—the gravel road; the dank buildings. Here there is restriction and the road leading into darkness brings attendant fear and trepidation. There is no room for change or growth or life. It could be summed up as a one-way street.

"You are challenged to obey and trust Me, having faith in My promises that My plan for your life is a good one. Do you decide to disobey and turn away from Me, your heart hardened and ignorant of My promises? Do you choose to fix your eyes firmly on yourself, living your life with no room for, nor realization of, the glorious plan I have created and designed you for?

"This is the challenge—yourself or Me first—My way, My truth, My life? The road of godly obedience leading to God's Kingdom starts out narrowly as you take up your Cross and live My way. Yet as you journey with and within Me, your knowledge and faith of the true meaning of that road begins to broaden—not towards fleshly destruction—but towards riches of spirit as you are lifted up, strengthened, encouraged, stretched, and challenged; as you are loved and cared for and ministered to in the deepest and truest way by your Savior and Creator of all there is.

"The choice is simple. Life—and life abundantly with Me—or death— and death eternal without Me. For I have overcome death with My willing sacrifice at the Cross—and your acceptance of My grace-drenched gift of forgiveness means that you overcome death also. No more battle between flesh and spirit. We live together in Paradise, in joyous praise and worship for all of Eternity."

> *Matthew 7:13*
> *"Enter through the narrow gate. For wide is the gate and broad is the road that leads to destruction, and many enter through it. 14 But small is the gate and narrow the road that leads to life, and only a few find it."*

> *1 Peter 4:16*
> *However, if you suffer as a Christian, do not be ashamed, but praise God that you bear that name. 17 For it is time for judgment to begin with God's household; and if it begins with us, what will the outcome be for those who do not obey the gospel of God?*

PERFECT ORDER;
PERFECT TIME

"My precious child. Allow yourself to surrender to My will for you, allow yourself to believe most truly that I have a plan for your life. I bring order to your chaos and all you need do is yield fully to Me.

"Surrender control to Me and allow Me to carry you. Your weakness is made strong within Me, your brokenness is made whole within Me, your pain and fear and confusion is healed within Me. And all the darkness and sorrow and intensity of aloneness becomes transformed by the power and security of My deep and total love for you. My love for you is higher, broader, deeper, and truer than you could ever imagine it to be.

"You are not alone. In all areas of your life I require your trust and your obedience, and the more you are able to trust and obey, the more you come to realize that I am with you and you never walk alone. Child of God, do not seek to withhold any parts of yourself from Me. For I know the intricacies of you; I know all the hidden places within the deepest part of your being. I see all the generations of your family stretched out in front of you and behind you. I see all of you! You cannot hide from Me—ever.

So realize that, even if you try to keep parts of you hidden, that it is impossible for this to be so. For I am your Creator, your Savior, and your God. I have given you My Holy Spirit to shine radiance into you at the deepest levels of your being. I have sent you My Holy Spirit to guide you, sustain you, and deliver you from the lies the enemy seeks for you to believe.

"Believe instead in Me, for I am total and absolute truth. No blemish. No tarnish. Only truth. Allow My truth in My name to breathe new life into you. Let the setting sun be as the closure of ways that are not of Me; ways that no longer serve you. Allow the promise of a new day dawning to be as a new beginning as you repent and give yourself to Me ever more fully.

"Step by step you journey with Me. With your heart seeking to serve Me and follow My ways, you press in closer to Me. This is the promise of our covenant relationship. I will never forsake you. You are never alone. My love for you is an assurance that every moment can be a new beginning in Me, in My perfect order and in My perfect time. Abide with Me."

Psalm 18:30
As for God, his way is perfect:
The LORD's word is flawless;
he shields all who take refuge in him.

Ecclesiastes 3:1
There is a time for everything, and a season
for every activity under the heavens.

DETAILED, INTRICATE, AND FEARFULLY WONDERFUL

"The same order and pattern and exquisite, intricate detail is present in every one of My creations. You as My creation need to understand this. My intention when I made you was to create a work that was detailed, intricate, and fearfully wondrous. And absolutely unique!

"And the pattern I have for your life, the plan I have made for My glory and your blessing, is just as unique, just as detailed, just as intricate, and just as fearfully wonderful. Yet you may not see this as yet. That you do not yet see is of no consequence. It is the truth as I have spoken of and promised in My Holy Scriptures.

"I willingly sacrificed My life at the Cross so that your sin could be washed clean and you could be free in My forgiveness. I ask that you also willingly sacrifice your life to Me. I ask that, if you believe in Me and trust Me, that you will also believe and trust what I say when I speak of how I see you and how I look upon you. You are My beautiful and precious child. Your humanity and My perfection go hand in hand and together we can accomplish all. All things are possible through Me. I strengthen you, I encourage you, guide you, and uplift you.

"Do not underestimate My creation—you!!!—and do not underestimate the power of My hand on your life. Do not believe the lies the enemy tries to steal your life away with. It is time to step boldly into the promises I have for you, to willingly surrender your control to Me, to glorify Me through the honoring of the gifts I have given you. It is time to love one another as I have loved you, to serve one another, and to forgive one another as I have forgiven you.

"All of this sets you truly free within Me. The life I have in mind for you is wonderful. It is time to believe and step forward into this. Step forward in faith, knowing I am with you every step that you take.

"So go boldly, child of God. Believe, trust, obey—and glorify Me with your life! I am with you always."

John 15:16
You did not choose me, but I chose you and appointed you so that you might go and bear fruit—fruit that will last—and so that whatever you ask in my name the Father will give you. 17 This is my command: Love each other."

Romans 8:1
Therefore, there is now no condemnation for those who are in Christ Jesus, 2 because through Christ Jesus the law of the Spirit who gives life has set you free from the law of sin and death. 3 For what the law was powerless to do because it was weakened by the flesh, God did by sending his own Son in the likeness of sinful flesh to be a sin offering. And so he condemned sin in the flesh, 4 in order that the righteous requirement of the law might be fully met in us, who do not live according to the flesh but according to the Spirit.

JOY AND FREEDOM

"Joy and freedom can be found in the simple pleasures of life that I as your Creator have designed for you—the pleasures which refresh your spirit, which nourish your spirit, and which lighten your spirit. A meal with loved ones. Laughter. Sunrise. Sunset. Swinging on a swing. A thousand other small and varied replenishments to your Spirit. Times where you allow yourself to collapse into the moment and lay down your burdens to enjoy the adventure and beauty of life!

"The day of rest is essential. Essential also are the times of rest sprinkled throughout each day. Make time for these. For you live life in this fallen world and there is much that is sorrowful and ugly, yet there is also much to celebrate and much that is beautiful.

"Seize the times where you celebrate living life on this earth in a way that is meaningful to you. Celebrate the very fact that I have given you breath! There is always something to be thankful for.

"Your one created life is supremely precious. Live it to the fullest, glorifying Me. Enjoy the adventure of being a child of God!"

> *Proverbs 15:13*
> *A happy heart makes the face cheerful,*
> *But heartache crushes the spirit.*

> *Ecclesiastes 8:15*
> *So I commend the enjoyment of life, because there is nothing better for a person under the sun than to eat and drink and be glad. Then joy will accompany them in their toil all the days of the life God has given them under the sun.*

IN HIS STRENGTH, NOT OURS

"Precious child of God. Know that I have gifted you with a heart that seeks to serve and help others. However, there is a danger that you would do this in your own strength. There is a danger that you believe that you can do for others and rescue them from that which they are challenged with. You cannot! Because you are not Me. I am the only One who can heal and transform pain and suffering permanently.

"Yet all are created with free will and there must be a *willingness* for pain to be faced and for healing to occur. This is a key understanding, My child. The understanding that there must be *willingness to face*, and *desire to heal*, past hurts. The willingness to face and bring all pain to Me, to My Holy Cross, for the guidance and the antidote to all trauma and damage. Only I can truly set the captives free, but there must be a willingness to look at what the bondages are. A willingness to break out of bondage, to tear down the strongholds formed within childhood and over generations. Fasting and prayer are vital in bringing these to the light, and skilled intervention with pastoral care can also assist.

"Yet first and foremost is willingness. You accepted Me and My gift of salvation willingly, and this willingness needs to continue to be chosen throughout our journey together. Willingness to trust and obey; willingness to live in the way I have laid out in My Holy Scriptures; willingness to heal pain that keeps the believer trapped and stifled. You became a new creation in Me when you accepted Me, yet pain and trauma may still be present within you, and this requires healing. I have promised a life that is full and rich with My blessing and this requires a willingness to work My way and dedicate all to Me.

"Follow My voice. Listen for My promptings from the Holy Spirit. Fast and pray. And be willing to do whatever it takes to be My disciple. For you belong to Me already, precious child, you were purchased for a price when I became a sin offering at the Cross. Yet I do not enslave you, but rather, in total surrender to Me, I set you free.

"So be willing to journey as I see fit, be aligned with My will. Be with Me."

John 14:23
Jesus replied, "Anyone who loves me will obey my teaching. My Father will love them, and we will come to them and make our home with them. 24 Anyone who does not love me will not obey my teaching. These words you hear are not my own; they belong to the Father who sent me."

Hebrews 12:1
Therefore, since we are surrounded by such a great cloud of witnesses, let us throw off everything that hinders and the sin that so easily entangles. And let us run with perseverance the race marked out for us, 2 fixing our eyes on Jesus, the pioneer and perfecter of faith. For the joy set before him he endured the Cross, scorning its shame, and sat down at the right hand of the throne of God. 3 Consider him who endured such opposition from sinners, so that you will not grow weary and lose heart.

TOTAL SURRENDER

"Surrender yourself totally to My way, My truth, and My life. Follow Me! Accept the simple yet profound position I am to occupy within your heart and mind. Total surrender. For I am at the center of every single moment of your existence and I require you to recognize this through your own free will.

"Beloved child, I am your breath, inward and outward. Enter into My stillness and then worship, praise, and adore Me as your Creator and Savior. Within this worship, praise, and adoration, the truth of who I Am begins to be revealed. Within this worship, praise, and adoration you are brought into My throne room and you remember that I am your King.

"Entering into this state of abandon and joy loosens the chains of fleshly desires that your fallen nature desperately seeks to cling onto. The worship and praise that you adore Me with is a means most powerful of transporting you into a higher realm. This realm is where the angels reside and where My Father and I live. Sing in adoration of Me, pray with abandon, speak to Me without censure, and thereby enter into a state of deeper communion with Me.

"You are lifted up spiritually as hands outstretch towards Me and voices are raised Heavenward in a sweetness of sound that delights My ears. Your songs of praise and joy and your prayers of thanksgiving and adoration move Me. We can be together in a way that is utterly powerful in its simplicity. Thoughts and the ceaseless chatter of the mind are switched off and the Holy Spirit comes in and moves powerfully through the believer. The spirit is renewed and replenished after such a time.

"So come before Me, My precious child, ready to adore Me. Know that I, your perfect and spotless Lamb of God, Deliverer of your soul, am ready to receive your praise and thanksgiving and to commune with you in a holy and worshipful celebration of who I am—your Lord, your King, your All in All. So sing—with abandon, giving yourself over to the power of praise and worship! Celebrate that I am here with you! Celebrate that I am alive! Celebrate that you belong to Me! Hallelujah!"

Psalm 47:6
Sing praises to God, sing praises;
sing praises to our King, sing praises.
7 For God is the King of all the earth;
sing to him a psalm of praise.

John 1:29
The next day John saw Jesus coming toward him and said, "Look, the Lamb of God, who takes away the sin of the world!

REFLECTION:
WE ARE WARRIORS
ON OUR KNEES

We are warriors on our knees, preparing to do battle using the power of prayer, in the full knowledge that the war is already won. We have victory in Christ Jesus. He fights our battles for us.

The mind is the scene for the spiritual battle yet the heart is the greatest weapon. A heart for Jesus and a longing to serve Him makes us strong warriors of faith. And the very best way to serve Jesus is to acknowledge our utter dependence on Him and to realize we must operate in His strength, not ours.

Let Jesus fight all of our battles for us. His heart is for us. His plan for us is good. He is glorified through the actions of His children. He is Lord of all and is as perfectly equipped for smaller fights as for full-scale battles. We do not need to be battle scarred and exhausted, weary from the onslaught of earthly life. We give all of this to Jesus Christ! He takes the burden from us.

Our role in the spiritual battle that is raging right here and now, through our serving hearts, is to be prayer warriors, communicating with Jesus through prayer, praise, and worship.

A prayer warrior learns to fight the spiritual battle by partnering with the Mightiest of Mighty, our Lord Jesus, through prayer requests and thanksgiving and praise for prayers answered. By praying without ceasing, we are teaming up with our Lord Jesus—and He is on the winning side!

Deuteronomy 3:21

At that time I commanded Joshua: "You have seen with your own eyes all that the LORD your God has done to these two kings. The Lord will do the same to all the kingdoms over there where you are going. 22 Do not be afraid of them; the LORD your God himself will fight for you."

Romans 7:23

but I see another law at work in me, waging war against the law of my mind and making me a prisoner of the law of sin at work within me.

SECTION 15

SAVE ME!

"All you need to do is cry out and reach out to Me, precious child of God. All this time I am right here, so close to you. Yet it may seem that I am on the other side of an ocean, so far away from you. It is a natural reaction to your circumstances to panic and feel overwhelmed. Yet, within your heart, with the noiseless words of the heart's cry, I ask you to cry out to Me. Reach for Me. I am then able to help you, to bring you to safety.

"So, My child, when you are feeling panicked and cannot find your way out of your desperation, cry out to Me within your heart. Say My name, 'Jesus,' as a soundless cry from your heart or as one which is loudly beseeching with your mouth. Either way, there is mighty power in My name, whether it is made with your sound or without. Come to Me and cling to Me by using My name as many times as you need. Each time, saying My name will give you more and more of My strength.

"I am close by, waiting for you to cry out to Me. Within your heart or with your mouth. My name. My powerful, eternal, redeeming, sanctifying name of pure love, of endless grace, of boundless forgiveness and mercy that cannot be measured. My name. Jesus!"

> *John 14:13*
> *And I will do whatever you ask in my name, so that the Father may be glorified in the Son. 14 You may ask me for anything in my name, and I will do it.*
>
> *Acts 4:29*
> *"Now, Lord, consider their threats and enable your servants to speak your word with great boldness. 30 Stretch out your hand to heal and perform*

signs and wonders through the name of your holy servant Jesus." 31 After they prayed, the place where they were meeting was shaken. And they were all filled with the Holy Spirit and spoke the word of God boldly.

ETERNAL WALK

"You will never stop walking with Me, for your eternal life is endless when you belong to Me. Live securely with the belief that your earthly life is short and each moment counts. To glorify Me you must live each moment as though it were the most precious moment in all of Eternity.

"I want that fire within you that giving yourself to Me truly ignites—for you to burn with the desire to serve Me and through My example, to serve your fellow man. I want you to live your life large and bold in your love for Me. I want you to embrace the God-given gifts I created within you. If you do not know what these are, pray for this to be revealed to you. Do not be ashamed of who I created you to be. Do not hide away. For I want My radiance to shine through you and for My light to brighten your countenance and fill up your being. I want you to trust in My promises and faithfully fix your eyes on Me. And allow My perfect love to cast out all your fear.

"Walk evenly with Me, yoked with Me. Give yourself over to Me. Let Me heal you. Not in the way that you always want, yet in the way that I know you need, in accordance with the intricate plan I have for your life. I cast out the darkness and the enemy is vanquished. Darkness can come in many forms—in the shape of doubts, fears, pain, torment, suffering, and pride, to name a few; anything which limits you and shrinks you, causing you to feel shame.

"I do not cause this—it comes straight from the enemy. I seek to expand you and uplift you. I will bring challenge to your life yet I promise that this challenge is bathed in love and My unfailing grace and mercy. Remember we are yoked and we walk together. I will never leave you nor forsake you. Ask for My help in all that you do, ask for My guidance and trust in Me. Ask in My name. I am your shield and protector against the lies and strife that the enemy wishes to burden you with.

"I created all that is, My precious child, and that I am well able to care for you goes without saying. My love for you is beyond your deepest dreams and imaginings. It is a love that saw Me willingly die on a Cross, as sin, so that we could be together for all Eternity. It is a love that will meet you on that glorious day when I bring you Home forever.

"I will wipe away all of your tears, My precious and beautiful broken child of God. And the adventure that began when you first gave yourself to Me will continue on in Paradise—yet glorious, rapturous, and perfect in every way. So look forward to that day, dearest child, knowing I go ahead to prepare a place for you. Rejoice and give thanks for where you are in your life right now, knowing I am also there with you there. Always with you."

> *Deuteronomy 31:8*
> *"The Lord himself goes before you and will be with you; he will never leave you nor forsake you. Do not be afraid; do not be discouraged."*

> *John 14:2*
> *My Father's house has many rooms; if that were not so, would I have told you that I am going there to prepare a place for you? 3 And if I go and prepare a place for you, I will come back and take you to be with me that you also may be where I am.*

HE KNOWS ME INSIDE OUT

"Lies and deception, a spirit of lack, a spirit of worthlessness—these are all of the enemy. They appear real but they are an illusion, without any substance whatsoever. The enemy has already lost the battle, yet he seeks to deceive and spread the pretense that this is not so. He does not even have one tiny miniscule speck of power against Me, not one!

"Your questions all have but one answer. My precious and cherished child of God, the answer is Me; the answer is My name—Jesus! Your Redeemer, your Deliverer, your Creator, your Savior! Name above all names. The power in My name thwarts all that the enemy attempts for evil.

"The power in My word spoke all into creation and being. If I say to you I have a plan for your life that is good, believe Me! My promises bloom all throughout Scripture—believe them! I am faithful and constant and I will anchor you firmly so you will not be tossed and turned by the ebb and flow of your circumstances. Believe me when I speak of how I want only the best for you—I who know you so thoroughly.

"So cast your cares on Me and delight in My presence! Be joyous and know that you are exactly where I need you to be, for your growth and My glory."

> *Isaiah 54:17*
> *"No weapon forged against you will prevail,*
> *and you will refute every tongue that accuses you.*
> *This is the heritage of the servants of the LORD,*
> *and this is their vindication from me,"*
> *declares the LORD.*

Luke 18:27
Jesus replied, "What is impossible with man is possible with God."

THE ADVENTURE OF LIFE

"I have measured out for you a certain number of breaths in your life. Live your life in full awareness of this and make each and every breath count. I have created a world of beauty for you and your wide open eyes can see everything there is on offer. There are many ideas, inspirations, and creative ventures for you to tap into. I walk with you always. My guidance allows you to navigate the pitfalls and seize the opportunities available when you live your life My way.

"You immerse yourself in Me, diving deep into the plan for your life that is created by Me and precious to Me. You take time to replenish through prayer and quiet time and to re-energize with praise and worship. Then you can dive back into what I have created you for, in order to glorify Me. The world for you as My child is a world of beauty and promise, challenge and learning. It is a life of adventure. Keep your eyes on Me and your eyes will be opened to see this. The enemy will try in vain to cloud or blind your vision but his attempts are no match for My love.

"So dive down, immerse yourself in this adventure of a life lived in faith, My cherished child of God, then come back up and replenish yourself as necessary. All within Me. Thankful to Me. Praising and worshiping Me. Listening to Me and speaking with Me. Resting in Me. Walking with Me. Always with Me. Together."

Colossians 2:6
So then, just as you received Christ Jesus as Lord, continue to live your lives in him, 7 rooted and built up in him, strengthened in the faith as you were taught, and overflowing with thankfulness.

GODLY FATHERING

"Every believer is a child of God and your Heavenly Father cares deeply for you, protecting and providing for you and making sure you have all that you need. This is the job of a father. Throughout My Holy Scriptures there are clear instructions for godly fathering.

"Godly fathers are so needed in this lost and hurting world that the enemy has claimed as his own. There are whole generations which have been bereft of a father's influence, whole generations where the role of father has been belittled and stripped back, weakened and made redundant. There are many fathers who have been absent from their children's lives—either physically through abandonment, or emotionally through abuse or incessant work life.

"A child is vulnerable and innocent and trusts his or her father. The effects of innocence destroyed and trust being violated and broken cannot be underestimated. The influence of a strong and secure father has repercussions through not just the immediate generation but generations to come. And the relationship a child has with his or her earthly father will usually be the way the relationship with his or her Heavenly Father is viewed.

"Yet I say to you that the relationship with your Heavenly Father is pure and perfect. There is no limit to My power and ability to heal and transform any wounds caused when earthly relationship is broken or damaged. My redeeming grace and forgiveness is what is needed to address and heal these wounds. Bring pain, unforgiveness, trauma, and unmet expectations to My Holy Cross, and pray and ask for Me to release and transform these with the power of My blood. Seek out the wise counsel of those people who are skilled in this area to assist you in this process.

"There is nothing that cannot be healed at My Holy Cross.

"So allow for the healing of these wounds, and also pray for godly men to be raised up as fathers, and for fathers who are lost and hurting and unsure of their role. Then pray for all to come into relationship with your Heavenly Father. Realize that you, when you became a child of God, were made innocent and blameless, forgiven and redeemed, when I became a ransom for your sins and at the Cross.

"And then, as the layers of pain and trauma are stripped away, you will find yourself able to begin to live as a child who can trust, a child who can have fun, a child who is secure and who is then willing and able to be obedient. A child of God who can look to their Heavenly Father as their protector and provider. For, as a child of God who journeys with Me, through healing and transformation, all of these qualities can be cultivated within you.

"So come unto Me as a little child, living in faith for that which you do not see, guided and loved for all Eternity by the One who gave you breath and who oversees every step you take. Come to Me now, My precious and treasured child of God. I am waiting to be with you."

> *Proverbs 22:6*
> *Start children off on the way they should go,*
> *and even when they are old they will not turn from it.*

> *Isaiah 54:13*
> *All your children will be taught by the LORD,*
> *and great will be their peace.*

OUR ROCK AND
OUR SECURITY

"You know from Scripture that I have overcome the world. I say to you that this overcoming is also available for you. The more you practice giving your worries to Me, praying without ceasing, and trusting and obeying Me, the less you will be attached to circumstances in this lost and fallen world. You fix your eyes on Me and I become your rock and your security, keeping you anchored in your faith and within Me. My Holy Word never varies. My promises are constant. My character is faithful. I am the only certainty in a fallen world of change—good and bad change, challenge and turmoil.

"Lean *on* me and lean closely *into* me. Stay close to Me by keeping the lines of communication open between us, praising Me, worshiping Me, praying to Me, listening for My voice and giving thanks to Me. Give thanks for the circumstances you find yourself in. No matter how it appears when you look at your circumstances through your natural eyes, you must put on your spiritual armor and look instead through your supernatural eyes. For in this moment you are precisely where I need you to be for your growth, within My goodness and grace and for My glory.

"Your circumstances, how I have created you, where I have placed you—all are necessary. Only I, the great I Am, hold all the pieces of the puzzle that is this point in your life. You can struggle and wish you were anywhere else. You can complain and wish you were anyone else. You are free to choose this way of struggle, but for what? You become exhausted by this approach very quickly. I say to you to instead cease the struggle, allow yourself to become quiet and still so that you may come before Me, realise that I am God, and simply surrender to Me, believing in faith that all is well.

"The more you cultivate this approach, the more you live your life My way. You become a spiritual warrior, fighting the good fight, overcoming the variables of circumstance, resting in Me and remaining constant within My eternal, unchanging, unwavering truth. This is My promise to you, My cherished child of God—that through your faith and belief in Me, you too are able to overcome the world. Rest in Me."

> *Deuteronomy 7:9*
> *Know therefore that the LORD your God is God; he is the faithful God, keeping his covenant of love to a thousand generations of those who love him and keep his commandments.*

> *Ephesians 6:10*
> *Finally, be strong in the Lord and in his mighty power. 11 Put on the full armor of God, so that you can take your stand against the devil's schemes. 12 For our struggle is not against flesh and blood, but against the rulers, against the authorities, against the powers of this dark world and against the spiritual forces of evil in the heavenly realms. 13 Therefore put on the full armor of God, so that when the day of evil comes, you may be able to stand your ground, and after you have done everything, to stand.*

REFLECTION:
THE ARROWS OF TRUTH
AND RIGHTEOUSNESS

Jesus is fully radiant in the Garden of Promise. Light of the most dazzling and pure emanates from Him. He is Radiance and Illumination. He is the Light of the World and the Light of Heaven. He is the Lord Jesus, sent to dispel all darkness.

Light illuminates that which is in shadow and secrecy; darkness and hiddenness. Jesus is this to this hurting and dark world. The enemy seeks to keep all hidden in deception and for darkness to shroud everyone in this fallen world. Jesus is the only One who is fully truth. His truth is the answer to transforming all that is so desperately lost in this fallen world. His way is sure and He is life itself. He is creation, Creator, and the Lord of the Universe.

Jesus' arrows of truth and righteousness pierce the heart of man with conviction. Yet some close themselves off to this; choosing to be hardhearted and seeking to set themselves up as their own god. They trust only what they see, hear, and sense. They walk in a world guarded and measured by having an answer to everything.

Yet to follow Jesus is to do the exact opposite to this in so many ways. For Jesus IS the answer to everything. Yet to come to Him requires a walk in faith, a trust in that which is unseen, a yielding to mystery and to a love so profound that it cannot be adequately described through words such as these.

Jesus chooses us to journey through this life and on towards Eternity. He transforms our hearts, refining us, purifying us, challenging us, disciplining us—loving us deeply and in an all-embracing way. His way is always for our best. His plan is always for His glorification and intricate in its detail of His goodness and grace.

We come to Him with praise, worship, thanksgiving, and readiness to obey Him. We follow Him.

Thank you, Jesus!

The Light of the World transforms us into the Children of Light.

> *Matthew 5:8*
> *Blessed are the pure in heart, for they will see God.*

> *Ephesians 5:8*
> *For you were once darkness, but now you are light in the Lord. Live as children of light 9 (for the fruit of the light consists in all goodness, righteousness and truth) 10 and find out what pleases the Lord. 11 Have nothing to do with the fruitless deeds of darkness, but rather expose them. 12 It is shameful even to mention what the disobedient do in secret. 13 But everything exposed by the light becomes visible—and everything that is illuminated becomes a light. 14 This is why it is said:*
> *"Wake up, sleeper,*
> *rise from the dead,*
> *and Christ will shine on you."*

SECTION 16

FREE WILL CHALLENGES

"Your fallen nature means that it is a challenge to follow the course of action which leads to Me. My commands are clear—to love Me with all that you have and to love your neighbor as yourself. Now with My Holy covenant of forgiveness at the Cross, divine relationship with Me can be re-established. However, it is still challenging to live My way.

"You speak words you do not wish to speak; you act as you do not wish to act; you doubt when you could live by faith; you are tempted and assailed by a multitude of worries and fears and shame.

"Yet I would say to you that, if you genuinely repent of your actions and set your course back towards Me, that I will stretch you and work with you until your race is run and you come Home to Me for Eternity. Until then, continue to strive to live My way, and when you slip up and act or speak in a way that is not honoring of Me, realize this and quite simply, repent. Genuinely repent.

"Be very aware of your thoughts as the seed of your actions. Keep a check on your thoughts. Reading My Holy Scriptures regularly, as a habit, will reframe your thought patterns and shine light on those thoughts that come from the enemy—the tormenting thoughts, the thoughts that incessantly steal your peace, the thoughts that are distracting and burdensome. I bring clarity of thought. So fix your eyes on Me, read My Scriptures, praise and worship Me, and speak to Me in prayer. This will clean up your thought life. Then there is much less possibility of thoughts which lead to impure actions.

"Make sure you regularly spend time with other believers, praying for and encouraging each other. Spending time only with non-believers can result in temptations of varying degrees. Flee from these temptations; do not try to withstand them. They also come from the enemy. God will never tempt you, only the enemy.

"Realize, precious child, that your life in this fallen world is set on a battlefield. This battle is a spiritual one. Yet, with prayer and a life given to Me, the battle is no longer yours to fight but is given over to Me. You are a warrior for God, praying and fighting with His full armor of prayer to vanquish the enemy who is already defeated. So rise up to this challenge, cherished child of God, and know that your victory is in Me, in Christ Jesus, your Redeemer, your Overcomer, your Creator and Savior. Your victory is in Me!"

> *Romans 7:15*
> *I do not understand what I do. For what I want to do I do not do, but what I hate I do.*

HE KEEPS HIS PROMISES

"My precious child. To live now, by faith, knowing that in a little while, you will be with Me in Paradise, is to commit to living with an intensity of purpose to glorify Me. Be focused on discovering and using your gifts for your goodness and My glory.

"This day in your life will never come again. Each moment is absolutely precious, and each thought and every action is a unique opportunity to glorify Me. You are made in the image of God, so it is your responsibility and privilege as His child to streamline your thoughts and actions to honor Him.

"Take up your Cross and follow Me. Lose yourself in worship and service to Me and you will find yourself as part of the body of Christ, involved and uplifted into a pure joy that is without limit. I guide and direct your footsteps and they all lead to Me. I am the Alpha, the Omega, the beginning and the end. I am the All in All. I Am. You are My promised and most precious child and I will keep you in the safety of My Shepherd protection, shielded and strengthened by My love and mercy, My forgiveness and grace.

"Long before you chose Me, I chose you, dearest child of God. Let us continue to choose each other in a life where you can be free within Me. Rest in Me."

Isaiah 41:10
So do not fear, for I am with you;
do not be dismayed, for I am your God.
I will strengthen you and help you;
I will uphold you with my righteous right hand.

Romans 8:28
And we know that in all things God works for the good of those who love
him, who have been called according to his purpose.

TEARING DOWN THE WALLS

"The walls of Jericho, which appeared impenetrable, came crumbling down when My instructions were followed. My precious child, you are to look at the walls you have built in your life which keep Me from being with you. The walls of idolatry, the walls of unforgiveness and resentment, the walls of isolation—any of these strongholds will keep you from fully entering My rest.

"Come before Me in repentance and, with a freshness of Spirit, pray to Me for My revelation and truth to shine the light on these places of darkness. With a repentant heart and a mind, body, and Spirit which seeks Me and My ways, these strongholds will crumble and disintegrate. I will enter where they have been.

"I have sent My Holy Spirit to guide you and give you discernment, and when you pray for your spiritual eyes to be opened and for your ears to truly hear, you begin to be able to journey ever more closely with Me. I provide the true security from which good decisions can be made.

"There are situations that may appear to be of Me in this fallen world, but which most surely are not. For the enemy attempts to trap and imprison you in the chains of deception. This deception can be small or monumental—no matter. Deception is deception. All deception is halted by a simple decision to turn back towards Me, to re-focus all that you do fully on Me and fully within Me.

"Remember this, My precious child, that your race is run with Me and for Me. I run every step of the way with you. Keep your eyes fixed firmly on Me and all truth will be revealed to you in accordance with this.

"Abide with Me. Settle for nothing less than this."

Joshua 6:1
Now the gates of Jericho were securely barred because of the Israelites.
No one went out and no one came in. 2 Then the LORD said to Joshua,
"See, I have delivered Jericho into your hands, along with its king and its
fighting men.

Luke 5:31
Jesus answered them, "It is not the healthy who need a doctor, but the sick.
32 I have not come to call the righteous, but sinners to repentance."

YOUR REDEEMER LIVES!

"My precious child. I ask you to allow more of Me and less of the idea that if you could change one part of your life, then the rest of your life would also change into *your* idea of perfection. And you would be anywhere other than where you are right now. Stop this!

"You are unable to see your situation from My point of view. If you were able to, you would surrender to your imperfect brokenness, realizing that for Me, it is actually the most beautiful part of you. I delight in giving you My strength in knitting your broken pieces back together. I delight in having you lean into Me. I delight when you collapse into Me. I delight in you knowing that you are My child and I am your God. Take delight in Me.

"You have to know that you are exactly *where* you need to be. You have to know that you are exactly *who* you need to be. The eyes you are seeing yourself through at this time are the eyes of criticism, regret, lack, and second guessing. You know who they originate from. Certainly not from Me. I am here to tell you that you have no need of this harsh approach to who you are and where you are.

"I am here to ask you, My cherished child, to let go of your judgment on your life and allow Me to take care of your situation. You are to fix your eyes on Me, do not let them waver for an instant, and walk with Me by faith. Step by step by step by step.

"Sometimes we will run, other times we will be skipping, sometimes we will be strolling, other times we will be crawling. And sometimes I will be carrying you. Only know that never will you be alone. Not for one instant. Believe in Me and know this to be true. I cannot lie to you.

"So take some time now to worship Me, praise Me as your Redeemer. For I delight in you and the plan that I have for your life. Allow it to unfold as I have designed it to unfold. Allow yourself to rest in the love that I have for you. Be still now."

Numbers 23:19
God is not human, that he should lie, not a human being, that he should change his mind. Does he speak and then not act? Does he promise and not fulfill?

2 Corinthians 12:9
But he said to me, "My grace is sufficient for you, for my power is made perfect in weakness." Therefore I will boast all the more gladly about my weaknesses, so that Christ's power may rest on me. 10 That is why, for Christ's sake, I delight in weaknesses, in insults, in hardships, in persecutions, in difficulties. For when I am weak, then I am strong.

A CLEANSING BALM

"Precious child. A part of you was taken by the enemy and seemingly destroyed. The lie he had you believe was that it was somehow your fault that abuse happened to you. If you had been another way—for in your eyes you were less than and lacking—then would this abuse have occurred?

"I am here to tell you that the enemy seeks to steal and kill and destroy—that is his purpose. It has nothing to do with who I have created you to be. You are My child, most precious and beautiful, and wholly worthy of respect and love. I ask now that you give Me back the part that the enemy sought to destroy, but which still lives, hidden and locked away. Together we can lovingly reclaim that which was lost and rebuild that which was shattered on that far off day so long ago.

"Let your tears fall, cherished child, for your tears are healing and cleansing. Let the control you have held onto for so long slip away into My loving embrace. Allow Me to occupy the space where once the darkness held you captive. You do not need to fully remember nor understand what occurred. It was done to you, perpetrated upon you, and you were unable to defend against it or stop it. That in no way reflects on your worth.

"You can be angry at Me for it happening to you. Yet I know who I am. I know who you are. I know and promise this in My Holy Scripture— that I turn all things evil for good. Your distress and your pain is something that I weep over, precious child. Yet I see all of the plan I have for you and the healing can come for others through the pain and suffering you have experienced.

"You have walked a journey that gives you compassion and empathy for others who have just begun on this most difficult pathway. I ask that you welcome your suffering, embrace your suffering, and give it all to Me. Hold fast to your faith. The enemy is vanquished already and has no hold over you.

"Rest now, My beautiful one, and know that your healing has been ongoing and will ebb and flow as your life progresses. Yet I remind you that you can give all parts of your pain to Me, to be washed clean at the foot of My redeeming and Holy Cross. Forgive all aspects of this situation and be free in the forgiveness I wrapped you in on that long-ago day when I died for you. For out of the ashes of death I rise, glorious and victorious, and so, My precious child, shall you rise too. In Me, For Me, with Me.

"I offer the truest freedom to you—freedom from the people and the circumstances of this world to determine who you are and who you will be. For I have overcome the world! Freedom from the lies the enemy has perpetrated on you and whispered into you. You have believed a lie if you have believed in any way that you are "less than."

"I care for you and I celebrate your glorious weakness, My precious child. For in your weakness you are strong. Your identity is now firmly within Me. Hold fast to Me and My promises, for I am the rock and anchor for you always. So come to Me, cherished child of God, and lay down your burden. Come to Me, for I will give you rest and comfort and healing and solace. Abide with Me."

> *Psalm 107:19*
> *Then they cried to the Lord in their trouble,*
> *and he saved them from their distress.*
> *20 He sent out his word and healed them;*
> *he rescued them from the grave.*
> *21 Let them give thanks to the Lord for his unfailing love*

and his wonderful deeds for mankind.
22 Let them sacrifice thank offerings
and tell of his works with songs of joy.

Philippians 3:7
But whatever were gains to me I now consider loss for the sake of Christ.
8 What is more, I consider everything a loss because of the surpassing
worth of knowing Christ Jesus my Lord, for whose sake I have lost all
things. I consider them garbage, that I may gain Christ 9 and be found in
him, not having a righteousness of my own that comes from the law, but
that which is through faith in Christ—the righteousness that comes from
God on the basis of faith. 10 I want to know Christ—yes, to know the
power of his resurrection and participation in his sufferings, becoming like
him in his death, 11 and so, somehow, attaining to the resurrection from
the dead. 12 Not that I have already obtained all this, or have already
arrived at my goal, but I press on to take hold of that for which Christ
Jesus took hold of me.

WASHING MY FEET

"It is time, My precious child, to treat yourself as lovingly and tenderly as I do. It is time to stop the judgment of yourself and the need to be in control. Give the control to Me.

"This is a time of healing for you, a time of allowing fragility, humility, and vulnerability. Call on My name to assist you in this process. Give your pain to Me and as I wash your feet, allow Me to wash all of you clean and clear with My Holy blood, shed for the forgiveness of your sins at My Cross.

"Give the thoughts of destruction to Me. Let yourself be free in Me. You are like a tiny seedling at this moment, which needs tender loving care to help it to grow. So take this time to let Me tend to your wounds, precious child of Mine, and allow others in to minister to you also. Allow support.

"Stay close to Me through reading My word, through prayer and supplication, through fasting, praise and worship, and fellowship. This is a season of gentleness yet immense power, as the stronghold of pain and devastation that has held you captive for so long is crushed by the mighty love and redemption of your Savior and Creator.

"I am the Lord Jesus Christ, your Comforter, your Savior, your Redeemer."

> *John 13:3*
> *Jesus knew that the Father had put all things under his power, and that he had come from God and was returning to God; 4 so he got up from the meal, took off his outer clothing, and wrapped a towel around his waist. 5 After that, he poured water into a basin and began to wash his disciples'*

feet, drying them with the towel that was wrapped around him. 6 He came to Simon Peter, who said to him, "Lord, are you going to wash my feet?" 7 Jesus replied, "You do not realize now what I am doing, but later you will understand."

REFLECTION:
OH! TO BE WITH
YOU, LORD JESUS!

Oh! To be with You, Lord Jesus! To be caught up in the air and to be with You in Your radiant and vast glory! To see Your glorious and magnificent face gazing at my own! To walk with You, commune with You, be with You, praise You, and thank You endlessly for giving me my life on earth and my life in Heaven with You. For a thin veil separates the two realms. Heaven and earth are so close together, separated only by the sting of death. And to live with you in Eternity is the promise that the sting of death has been overcome.

I cannot imagine anything more wondrous than being in Heaven with you, Lord Jesus. The vivid colors, the myriad angels, the children of God raised and perfected in their new bodies, the endless praise and worship, the mansion with its room set aside just for me and, permeating everything, the absolute, unending joy. And my fervent desire and wish is to see my family and loved ones come to You and come to know You so that they may live in Heaven also.

So grant in me, Lord Jesus, the prayers that will draw these people to You; shine Your light through me so that I may be a messenger and an empty vessel filled with Your Holy Spirit to shine the light of the gospel into the hearts of those who live in this unbelieving world. I pray these unbelievers will turn to You, Lord Jesus, turn to You, that they will open up their hearts wide and that all may come to You.

Praise be Your name, in Your mighty name of Jesus. Hallelujah. Amen.

Isaiah 25:1
LORD, you are my God; I will exalt you and praise your name,

for in perfect faithfulness you have done wonderful things, things planned long ago.

1 Timothy 2:1
I urge, then, first of all, that petitions, prayers, intercession and thanksgiving be made for all people—2 for kings and all those in authority, that we may live peaceful and quiet lives in all godliness and holiness. 3 This is good, and pleases God our Savior, 4 who wants all people to be saved and to come to a knowledge of the truth. 5 For there is one God and one mediator between God and mankind, the man Christ Jesus, 6 who gave himself as a ransom for all people. This has now been witnessed to at the proper time.

SECTION 17

CLEARING A HEAVY SPIRIT

"Each day is a new beginning, blessed in My name, holy and fresh and restorative. Within that day, each second, each minute, each hour are all opportunities to begin again in Me. Precious child, do not become bogged down by poor choices and decisions you make—for they can become strongholds within your mind, and soon your thinking process becomes cloudy and heavy.

"Repentance is the key to clearing a heavy spirit. Turn towards Me with a heart full of repentance and your spirit will be cleansed and uplifted, your heart will be refreshed, and you will be granted a new page to begin again on. Forgiveness was given to you at My Cross and your sins were remembered no more.

"Repentance is your willingness to admit your trespasses and give back to Me that which clouds our relationship. For your sins have been forgotten by Me, yet your fallen nature still exists. You are human, precious child, forgiven and sanctified, yet still responsible and accountable for the human choices you make.

"My forgiveness is renewable each second, each moment, each day. Your part in this is to genuinely repent, turn back to Me, and be cleansed and refreshed with My living water and My promise of freedom.

"Peace be with you."

> *Lamentations 3:22*
> *Because of the LORD's great love we are not consumed, for his compassions never fail. 23 They are new every morning; great is your*

faithfulness. 24 I say to myself, "The LORD is my portion; therefore I will wait for him." 25 The LORD is good to those whose hope is in him, to the one who seeks him.

Acts 3:19

Repent, then, and turn to God, so that your sins may be wiped out, that times of refreshing may come from the Lord, 20 and that he may send the Messiah, who has been appointed for you—even Jesus. 21 Heaven must receive him until the time comes for God to restore everything, as he promised long ago through his holy prophets.

FRAGILE AS FINE CHINA

"Your heart is the most vulnerable yet the strongest organ of your body. It is fragile as fine china in the area of emotions; able to be cracked so easily. Yet it is also the strongest and most vital part of your body. Life is not sustained for very long once the heart stops beating. Physically, your life force is contained within your heart and emotionally, your ability to open up to life is also contained within it.

"I look at your heart as the way in which you lead and reach out to others. What is most vulnerable and open to being hurt is also your greatest strength. It is the pure intent of your heart which reaches others and it is your heart that I am remaking moment by moment into the likeness of Me.

"Your heart is so important! It sustains life. I hold your heart now; you gave it to Me when I set you free. I began to remake your heart when I set you free, I began to renovate it and rework it. I gave you a new perspective to lead with your heart. So open yourself up wide and have a heart for Me and a heart to serve others, just as I taught when I walked the earth and just as My Holy Spirit guides you now.

"Love is the greatest force known to mankind and the force of My love is greatest of them all—it is the redemptive, regenerative, refreshing type of love that can transform lives. I was given in love to this world to save it and see it free. I work through all of My children to spread My message of hope and transformation, to model Christ-like service and to love their fellow man.

"So lead with your heart, precious child. Do not close it off because of emotional hurts. Open it up to the love of Christ, which is the balm for all emotional hurts and wounding. Let My love for you prevail in all that you say and do. In My Precious, Mighty, and Holy Name above all Names."

Ezekiel 36:26
I will give you a new heart and put a new spirit in you; I will remove from you your heart of stone and give you a heart of flesh.

Mark 12:30
Love the Lord your God with all your heart and with all your soul and with all your mind and with all your strength.' The second is this: 'Love your neighbor as yourself.' There is no commandment greater than these."

HOLY SPIRIT; SOULISH URGES

"The sword of My truth cut your soul asunder from your Spirit on the day I set you free. Now My Holy Spirit lives in you as your guide and your Comforter, illuminating My Holy Word of Scripture and giving you revelation upon revelation of My unending love. Your soul still exists within you as the natural part of you, yet as you are led by the Spirit, this soulish part of you yields more and more to the likeness of Christ that is growing within you.

"You walk in faith, led by the Holy Spirit now, yet soulish urges still clamor for space. Do not fear, precious child! Keep focusing on My Word, keep your eyes fixed on Me, and you become less and less driven by what your soul is wanting. Being led by the Spirit means praying for guidance from the Holy Spirit in My Holy name.

"As you are filled up with the Holy Spirit and bow in obedience to Me, less and less are you apt to be swayed by your soul urges. More and more you are made into My image. More and more you surrender to being part of the Body of Christ. You are uniquely created and crafted by My master hand, yet you are made to be in fellowship and relationship and function as part of the whole, part of Me and indwelt by My Holy Spirit.

"The isolation of your soul becomes less and less as more and more you become Spirit filled. You worship in the Spirit, your thoughts are of the Spirit, you have the discerning will of the Spirit. Know this, surrender to this, and submit to this fully.

"Come unto Me."

John 4:24
God is spirit, and his worshipers must worship in the Spirit and in truth.

Hebrews 4:12
For the word of God is alive and active. Sharper than any double-edged sword, it penetrates even to dividing soul and spirit, joints and marrow; it judges the thoughts and attitudes of the heart.

COLLAPSE INTO JESUS

"I know the struggles you have. I know the times you want to lay down and never get up again. I know the times you want to close yourself off from every outside influence and retreat back into that hiding place. The times when you are in the grip of depression. And the grip can become tighter and tighter, squeezing the life out of you like a vice. You can lose sight of all but the depression.

"I ask you to look at your depression in its most literal meaning. A depression is a ridge, an indentation, a hollow. I ask that you substitute Me for your depression. I am the ridge, the indentation, the hollow for you to lean into. Since I walk with you through the Valley of Death, I am He you can safely collapse into. I am He who you can relinquish everything to; who you can rest within for as long as you need. I am He who you can close yourself off to. And I am He who is your refuge; your safety; your hiding place from the fallen world.

"I am the depth of darkness made light again. I am the antidote to the poison of paralyzing self-doubt. I am the victor in the battle of the mind. I am the healer of your tender heart. Give your depression to Me and allow Me to heal it. Pray for My sovereign power to work in you; listen for My instructions, and be guided where necessary to the correct people and treatments to assist you.

"For the battle in the mind is an ongoing one. Rely on My promises for you and allow Me to apply what is needed for you. For I am your Creator, your miracle-working God; you are My precious child. I am vast and majestic; your depression is not. Give it all to Me. Rest in Me."

Exodus 23:25
Worship the LORD your God, and his blessing will be on your food and water. I will take away sickness from among you.

Hebrews 7:25
Therefore he is able to save completely those who come to God through him, because he always lives to intercede for them.

MADE FOR RELATIONSHIP

"You were created not to live in isolation, but in fellowship and companionship. For each one of My creations there is a helpmate. Be focused on Me and also on others be focused, and I promise you rich relationship. You do not need to think about this, nor worry, nor fret about this. It is a given. You were made for relationship.

"Reach out to others when you are listening to the enemy's attempts to persuade you otherwise. Pour out your isolation, your aloneness, your sorrow, and your self-loathing onto Me. I can take it all from you. I am more than equipped. For, if left to fester inside of you, it keeps you from being all I created you to be. The enemy's lies are an illusion. My Scripture is truth. So look at and to My Scripture. Believe in the plans I have for you.

"You are not alone. You are My child. I have given My life for you. I love you endlessly, with a protection and a fervor that is unmatched. You are My creation. I have gifted you uniquely. Give to Me that which is not of Me and I will wash it clean and fill the space within you that these lies used to occupy. My love for you and relationship with you is an eternal one—nothing can separate us.

"I am spring cleaning your house, precious child, making it fresh and new for renewed beginnings. So rest, be gentle and protective of the love that I have given you, the love that will set you free. Be in relationship with Me, turn to Me, yield to Me, give to Me all that does not serve you. Ask what is of Me, and whatever is not, pray in My name for Me to release you from it; to set you free from its bondage.

"You were created for freedom, joy, relationship, and glorification of Me. Embrace this destiny and recognize that it is My handiwork. For I love you and My forgiveness and mercy has set you free."

Nahum 1:7
The LORD is good, a refuge in times of trouble. He cares for those who trust in him.

Revelation 4:11
"You are worthy, our Lord and God, to receive glory and honor and power, for you created all things, and by your will they were created and have their being."

SMASHING THE STRONGHOLDS

"All that you see is limited to your own vision. Yet lift your eyes to Me! I can assure you that My vision is without limit; I Myself am unlimited. I am bigger than anything you can imagine. My abilities are vaster than you can hope to realize.

"This is where you must trust My word, trust the relationship we build together, and trust the journey we are on. This is where you must be obedient even unto death to Me. My perfection works with your brokenness. I lift you up into the palm of My mighty hand and I hold you there, protected, nurtured, sheltered, and anointed.

"So give to Me all that is hidden within you. Ask that I shine My radiant light into and onto that which is not known to you and comes from the enemy. Ask for Me to smash and crush the strongholds and idolatry that have kept you in bondage; trapped to be less than who I created you to be. You are made in My image of love, power, truth, and service; you are made for My glorification. The enemy lies to you and seeks for you to be trapped within a life of fear, envy, weakness, lies, and selfishness; allowing him to steal and destroy, believing you are less than: inconsequential, powerless and useless, made to be alone and isolated.

"Yet, My precious child, know this—that you are made in My image— you are part of Me, part of the body of Christ, you are My chosen, cherished, justified, sanctified, forgiven masterpiece. And as part of Me I complete you; as part of Me you are designed for rich and deep relationship with Me. I have made you unique with gifts and temperament, personality and appearance that are totally one of a kind. Yet you are created to be in relationship with Me and were never meant to be alone. I designed you to be celebrated as My creation, as part of

Me. I celebrate your birth unto Me, dear child! And I have a Plan for you that is designed to make you prosper in every way imaginable and far beyond what you can know at this time.

"So pray and ask Me to take the fear, the lack, the isolation, the idolatry, and all those hidden strongholds from you. Ask Me to take all that hinders My plan for you to come to fruition. Repent of any pride that has kept you from coming before My throne of grace. And realize, dearest child, that I have forgiven you. That you were forgiven at My Holy Cross. My grace is unlimited. My mercy is unlimited. I am just and I am faithful. I am Holy, Holy, Holy. I have made you fearfully and wonderfully. Realize that I am the victor and that in Me, you are victorious.

"Allow for My freedom to come into you and bind those strongholds Satan had you believing were you. Ask for this to be so in My Holy, Mighty, Name above all Names. Jesus.

"And believe this. Walk in faith. With Me. I love you in this world and in the Eternity beyond. And you belong to Me. Go in peace."

> *2 Corinthians 10:4*
> *The weapons we fight with are not the weapons of the world. On the contrary, they have divine power to demolish strongholds. 5 We demolish arguments and every pretension that sets itself up against the knowledge of God, and we take captive every thought to make it obedient to Christ.*

REFLECTION:
ANGELS OF LIGHT

I can see millions of angels glowing incandescently, surrounding me and lifting their angelic voices in a chorus of praise and worship. This is happening constantly in the Heavenly realms. Whenever a believer comes to Christ the angels shout for joy—unparalleled joy and celebration, exultation and exuberance. Another soul is safely with the King! The angels intercede and protect; they keep watch and battle with the forces of darkness who would wish to overtake unknowing souls.

Even Satan himself can be disguised as an angel of light. But the real angels are those who serve Jesus, Lord Jesus, Lord of all creation and the Savior of the world. They can appear as people and walk among humankind. They can point people towards Jesus and make His name be known.

So give where there is a need. For you never know when an angel, in the service of our Lord, can come into contact with you. Feed the hungry, clothe and shelter those who are lacking. Do this for the least of those so that your Father may know you glorify Him.

And when you praise and worship Lord Jesus, be aware that you are adding your voice, lifting your voice, to join with the multitudes in Paradise, who constantly, unceasingly, adore their Lord. And let this knowledge fill you with joy and humility. We serve a great and faithful God, a spotless and most worthy Lamb of God. Sing Hallelujah!

Luke 15:10

In the same way, I tell you, there is rejoicing in the presence of the angels of God over one sinner who repents.

Revelation 12:7

Then war broke out in heaven. Michael and his angels fought against the dragon, and the dragon and his angels fought back. 8 But he was not strong enough, and they lost their place in heaven. 9 The great dragon was hurled down—that ancient serpent called the devil, or Satan, who leads the whole world astray. He was hurled to the earth, and his angels with him.

SECTION 18

YOUR PRECIOUS HEART

"Precious child, you are to focus on Me with your whole heart. Each action you undertake, focus on Me with your whole heart. Distractions will come in and seek to shift that focus from Me; refocus with your whole heart on Me.

"Ask for a heart that chases after Me, that yearns for Me and My Word, that seeks to make a difference in this world in My Holy Name. For I have your heart now, it is captive to Me, I remake your heart second by second, minute by minute, hour by hour, day by day—and onwards as we journey towards Eternity and the time when your heart will burst open and come Home to Me.

"Your precious heart is what I look at; you cannot hide what is in your heart from Me. I know all that is within your heart. You may not. So ask for what I have placed inside your heart to be revealed to you. In My name, ask for the desires of your heart to be revealed to you. And step out boldly in faith to follow these. For these are your gifts; these are the desires of your heart. These are not your needs, no, for I take care of your needs naturally. These are your desires, the deepest stirrings of what I created you to give to your world. These are large and bold and not designed for you to create in your humanness. They are designed for you to create within Me; with Me and in My strength.

"They are supernatural in their scope and they require a Spirit of boldness and a faith and belief in My abilities; not your own. For your gifts from Me require My abilities and My vastness and majesty to bring them wholly into your world. Your gifts are not dependent on your ability to bring them to fruition. I require that you trust Me so that I can work with you in My strength, not yours, to fulfill My Plan. I want you utterly dependent upon Me! I want your every thought to be captive to Me!

"Most of all, I want your heart to be softened towards Me and humble unto Me so that what I am intending for you can then be poured out of your heart. It can spring from My living water that nourishes you and quenches your thirst. It can come from a realization that all has been done for you already at the Cross, and from this revelation you are then able to love most truly those who you come in contact with.

"So give Me your precious heart each and every day and pray for Me to make it pure and repentant, willing and open to do My bidding. For My glory, not yours, My precious child of God."

> *Psalm 37:4*
> *Take delight in the LORD,*
> *and he will give you the desires of your heart.*

> *Proverbs 4:23*
> *Above all else, guard your heart,*
> *for everything you do flows from it.*

BRAVE AND BOLD

"The Spirit of the Lord is upon you, precious child, when you call out to Me, when you earnestly seek My will, when you bring to Me all the doubts and fears and thoughts that plague and torment you.

"You ask Me is it prideful to want to let your talents shine? Is it prideful to want to make money from your gifts and share what I have given you with your world? You ask Me is it prideful to want to make a difference to your world and to dream large and big?

"Precious cherished child of God, I say to you that the motivation of the heart I have put into you is to bless others. I say to you to be brave and bold and let My glory shine into the places where darkness has dwelled for so long.

"You cannot be meek and timid and fulfil the boldness and bravery your gifting entails. You are afraid to step into what I have for you because you do not wish to appear big headed or prideful. But so long as you stay close with Me this will not happen. I want you to honor Me—and this cannot happen if you are afraid to step out and risk breaking free of the shell of fear you have encased yourself within.

"Fear, lack, timidity, minimizing of the gifts you have been given—these are prideful. When you live your life enslaved by these lies of the enemy, you are effectively saying you know better than I what your life should be. These lies from the enemy dissolve into nothing when you look to My promises and embrace them in a large way. Live life large. You do not need to minimize who I created you to be. Live life fully. You do not need to lessen anything about yourself. Dream big!!! For you are a masterpiece, My precious child. You are My creation. You are made for My glory.

"So let go. Give it all to Me—all that you are, all that I am calling you to be, all that I created you to be. Admit and surrender that you do not know what is best for you. Admit and surrender that you cannot cope. Admit and surrender you are powerless to create your life. Let life rush in to greet you, let My love fill you up and spill out of every pore of your skin—truly alive, living in technicolor, vivid, vital, pulsing and throbbing with the life force of My glory.

"Let the fear go by giving it to Me. Every time it raises its head and wants you to live tiny, give it to Me, your great and vast God, and let Me transform it.

"For you are so loved! You seek to do My will. You seek to be obedient. You earnestly desire to serve Me. So stay close with Me, dear one, and let us work this out together. Go in peace."

> *Psalm 127:1*
> *Unless the LORD builds the house,*
> *the builders labor in vain.*
> *Unless the LORD watches over the city,*
> *the guards stand watch in vain.*

COME WORK FOR ME!

"It is time to take up your Cross and follow Me. For when you are at the end of yourself, unable to do anything in your own strength—and able to recognize that your strength is not what your life in Me is about—is when you are at the beginning of Me.

"You are at the beginning of what I promise for you—a life of journeying with Me, a life of not just recognition of what I have done for you and all that I have for you, but a life of revelation of Me. Realize that your frailty and your inability to cope are what I require, so that you are dependent completely on Me. Realize that you have identified your abilities and your gifts as *yours* and this has been precisely what has kept you from Me. With this realization, you are then ready to journey with Me more deeply.

"So you take up your Cross—your realization that you are frail and broken yet so, so loved and cherished, My human child—and you follow after Me, you seek after My heart, you chase after all that I have for you. For I seek to pour out onto you blessing after blessing after blessing. Only realize that all you are and all you do is for My glory, for Me to grow you, for Me to deepen your faith, and for Me to bring you Home at the end of the race to come before My throne of grace and live with Me in Eternity.

"So come work for Me, become joyously busier than ever before, for Me and in Me. Do all for My glory, precious child. For this is freedom, true freedom. Freedom and forgiveness in Me, bathed and nurtured in My living water and redeemed with My unending love and grace. So yield to Me, precious one. Abide with Me."

2 Corinthians 8:5

And they exceeded our expectations: They gave themselves first of all to the Lord, and then by the will of God also to us.

Ephesians 6:7

Serve wholeheartedly, as if you were serving the Lord, not people, 8 because you know that the Lord will reward each one for whatever good they do, whether they are slave or free.

YOKED WITH JESUS

"I want you to see yourself as yoked with Me. That we are together all the time. You travel with Me in the palm of My hand, in safety and security. You check in with Me as to whether what you are hearing is from Me. I am the leader in your life, at the center of your life, to be glorified by all you do.

"Yet I also seek to serve you by guiding you and showing you the steps I wish you take. Each decision is to be made in obedience to Me; I require unceasing prayer and unending communion with Me. The spirit of boldness I am cultivating within you requires surrender to Me and to the radical way I require you to live. For My words are contrary in so many ways to the culture that you find yourself living within.

"There is no you and I any longer; it is us. You are not to put yourself first; you are to submit in obedience to Me. Yet this is a freeing submission; not an enslaving one. You are part of My body and I require you to recognize that all parts of the body work together as one coordinated whole. Each part is of vital importance and is necessary for the smooth running of the whole.

"And as you lose yourself within Me, cherished child of God, you begin to find the freedom I have promised. As My creation, you are made to be in relationship with others and with Me. And as you lose yourself in obedience to Me and honor Me with your faith and trust, you begin to break free of the shackles of this fallen world. The true nature of relationship between us, lost in the Garden of long ago, begins to be restored.

"There is deep mystery inherent in the harmony between you as My created one and Myself as your Creator. Only trust in My ability to be your God and have faith that the covenant forged at My Cross is everlasting. We journey together in a fallen world, precious child, but our journey does not end here. You are on the road to Eternity. And I am by your side—your loving, faithful, glorious Creator. You are My child and I am your God. Be with Me."

Job 22:21
Submit to God and be at peace with him; in this way prosperity will come to you. 22 Accept instruction from his mouth and lay up his words in your heart.

2 John 1:6
And this is love: that we walk in obedience to his commands. As you have heard from the beginning, his command is that you walk in love.

IT IS NOW WE

"My precious child! If you only had the eyes to see what I see when I look at you, My creation. You see your wounds, your brokenness or the damage you believe you are. Yet I see My child, made in My image. I see My child in glory with Me, at the end of the race, exultant to Me, living with Me in Eternity. I see you through the plan I have for you; I see how wondrously you have been fashioned; I have breathed My life into you first in your fallen nature and then again when you chose to come to Me.

"Nothing can separate you from Me, and in this truth realize, dearest cherished child, that you are now hidden within Me and you are not only My precious creation, but a sacred and redeemed part of Me. Your body is part of My body. My body was broken at the Cross and then glorified with My Father in Heaven—this is truth for you also, redeemed one. For the enemy's hold over you was broken at My Cross! You were given a new heart forged in the gift of forgiveness and you were set free from death's sting at that time also. A new creation was born and you, at the end of this walk on earth, will be reborn yet again into your new body and glorified with Me in Heaven above.

"So banish the thought of *you*, precious child, for it is now *we*. Your thoughts are with Me, your mind is with Me, your heart is with Me. You belong with Me and are within Me now.

"The Lord of the Universe claims you in victory!

"So believe now, and look upon yourself with the eyes of royalty and as one who is a child of the Most High King. It is time for this now.

"No more prideful lessening of who you are in Me. You are more than a conqueror. Be with Me, knowing I am love—redeeming, eternal love poured out through My healing blood at the Cross of Salvation. Go forward—forgiven, redeemed, justified, and sanctified! My creation!"

Luke 12:32
Do not be afraid, little flock, for your Father has been pleased to give you the kingdom.

Romans 8:16
The Spirit himself testifies with our spirit that we are God's children. 17 Now if we are children, then we are heirs—heirs of God and co-heirs with Christ, if indeed we share in his sufferings in order that we may also share in his glory. 18 I consider that our present sufferings are not worth comparing with the glory that will be revealed in us.

DYING TO SELF

"A kernel of wheat dies in order for it to produce a multitude of seeds. You are as that grain of wheat. When you begin to die to your old self and live My way, within you begins the transformation and the changing of your old fallen nature into a Christlike nature. The Christlike nature embraces and seeks to spread the gospel message and draws to itself new souls for the Kingdom. So the many come from the death of the one.

"My sacrifice at the Cross of Salvation was also a death of the one to produce a sowing and reaping of many. The forgiveness of sin as it was nailed to the Cross with Me brought the new covenant and the promise of a new relationship with Me under grace. All are able to come to Me.

"Continue to die to self each and every day. Pray for the way to be open to draw to you those who are searching. Be the kernel of wheat which dies so that the many seeds can spring forth. Allow your human personality to step aside so that the power of the Holy Spirit can give you the words needed to pour out its gospel message to those who are seeking.

"For those who are seeking will surely find the soil they require. Their tiny seed of seeking shall take root in the good soil and sprout into a faith in Lord Jesus. With the water of relationship with Christ and the sunshine of obedience to Him, the faith is then able to bloom and grow into a deep and abiding testament to God's eternal glory.

"Praise Him!"

John 12:24

Very truly I tell you, unless a kernel of wheat falls to the ground and dies, it remains only a single seed. But if it dies, it produces many seeds. 25 Anyone who loves their life will lose it, while anyone who hates their life in this world will keep it for eternal life. 26 Whoever serves me must follow me; and where I am, my servant also will be. My Father will honor the one who serves me.

Romans 6:4

We were therefore buried with him through baptism into death in order that, just as Christ was raised from the dead through the glory of the Father, we too may live a new life.

REFLECTION:
POWER IN THE BLOOD

The Cross is in the Garden. As I watch Jesus hanging there my heart is beating wildly. "Did there have to be this?" I am asking. "Did it have to be like this?" And the answer comes that this was but a speck within Eternity, but a speck so monumental as to change the order of the universe.

Jesus became sin. I move close so that the blood of my Jesus is dripping on me, and then it pours over me. It doesn't feel like blood, it feels like the purest rainwater, brighter and clearer than any water I have ever known. And Jesus comes down off that Cross to stand beside me—radiant, beautiful. He shows me His hands and feet just like He showed the apostles when He appeared to them after He had been resurrected. I can see the holes in His hands and feet.

I trace the outlines of them and my tears fall as I start to comprehend how much He loves me. *"There is power in My blood, it is the life force, the sustenance that is able to sustain and transform. Just like blood is carried throughout the body via veins, so too is My precious blood able to move throughout your body, healing and changing all that it touches."* Experiences, memories, pain, misunderstandings—all can be brought to the Cross of Jesus and transformed through the power of His blood washing these clean.

Jesus died on the Cross, but then He transcended death and rose again and He is alive now; so fully alive it is almost unbearable to comprehend! *"All can be taken to the Cross. Just as I finished sin I can finish all that keeps you from being in relationship with Me. Past, present, future—all can be washed and transformed with My precious, Holy, mighty blood."* There is power in the blood. In the blood of Jesus.

Jesus came down from the Cross at Calvary and into the hearts of men with His amazing grace, His sweet, redemptive, restorative grace, so that never again could the relationship between God and man be broken. Through His grace, He did it all. There is nothing more for us to do other than remember we are His and He is ours—and act accordingly.

> *Matthew 26:28*
> *This is my blood of the covenant, which is poured out for many for the forgiveness of sins.*

> *Revelation 1:5*
> *And from Jesus Christ, who is the faithful witness, the firstborn from the dead, and the ruler of the kings of the earth. To him who loves us and has freed us from our sins by his blood, 6 and has made us to be a kingdom and priests to serve his God and Father—to him be glory and power for ever and ever! Amen.*

SECTION 19

THE POWER OF PRAYER

"Of unseen might and power, with all things asked for in My mighty name, is the weapon of prayer. You are a prayer warrior, My child, and you fight with the weapon of prayer against unseen forces. The battle is in the spiritual realms for the children of God. For the battle is being waged as to who will come to salvation and who will be lost and dashed.

"The power of prayer is that it builds a bridge between yourself and your Heavenly Father. Instantly you are in His presence. His ear is always listening yet opens wider when He hears your fervent prayers. Praise His Mighty Name and thank Him most earnestly for all of the blessings and circumstances you find yourself placed within. Then ask Him for what you need; pray unceasingly in the mighty name of Jesus because it builds a wall of protection around you; it keeps your mind and heart on Him; it keeps you in humility, knowing that you can only do and be in His strength.

"Prayer changes everything; prayer confirms what you already know to be true—that Jesus is Lord. Your spoken words in prayer and the unspoken words from deep within your frail heart are both heard by your Father in Heaven.

"So praise, thank, and ask, and await in trembling for your prayers to be answered. In My will and perfect time, not yours; for I have all the pieces of the puzzle, which is the good Plan for your life. Submit in obedience and believe that your Father desires to bless you in accordance with what He is teaching you. He is refining you like silver in a furnace and all that is not needed must be burned off first. So trust in the way of the Lord.

"Pray for your Father's will in your life. Pray for obedience. Pray with thanksgiving that all that He has for you will be revealed to you. Be alive in Him and your prayers will become a communion between you, a time of sacredness as your heart fills with the joy of His presence. He seeks for you, all of you, and so you can come to Him secure in the knowledge that He will welcome you.

"Blessed be the Lord our God!!!

> *2 Chronicles 7:14*
> *If my people, who are called by my name, will humble themselves and pray and seek my face and turn from their wicked ways, then I will hear from heaven, and I will forgive their sin and will heal their land. 15 Now my eyes will be open and my ears attentive to the prayers offered in this place. 16 I have chosen and consecrated this temple so that my Name may be there forever. My eyes and my heart will always be there.*

> *Colossians 4:2*
> *Devote yourselves to prayer, being watchful and thankful. 3 And pray for us, too, that God may open a door for our message, so that we may proclaim the mystery of Christ, for which I am in chains. 4 Pray that I may proclaim it clearly, as I should. 5 Be wise in the way you act toward outsiders; make the most of every opportunity. 6 Let your conversation be always full of grace, seasoned with salt, so that you may know how to answer everyone.*

CHILD OF LIGHT

"Each of you shine the light of My glory in the world. These collective lights point towards My greater illumination and radiance. Together, the light from the many illuminates the light of the One. Do not underestimate the power of your contribution as being a child of light. The world is so full of darkness—fear, greed, poverty, rape, murder, idolatry, and so much more in this fallen world. Yet the light will always dispel the darkness. In a darkened room, the light from one candle provides a radiance that brightens the whole of that room.

"Remember this—you are calling forth the light in My name to dispel the power of the darkness that the enemy calls forth. People who cannot see where they are going need the light to shine the way. Be that light. It is never easy to keep the light from a candle glowing, but if you place the light into a lampstand, it has protection. I am the lampstand and the light.

"I offer and provide protection in Me for all My children. The enemy cannot for one second withstand My might. He is a counterfeit! He was banished to fallenness for wanting to be God, so he seeks to undermine all that is of God, all that is precious and pure and perfect. He hates God's children with a vengeful and cruel fervor. His obstacles may appear real but they are counterfeit; an illusion just as he is.

"So, My child of light, continue to be the light that shines forth from My grace and for My glory. Point your light towards Me. Pray with fervor as the time for the light of the world to return draws closer. Abide with Me."

MEREDITH SWIFT

Psalm 119:105
Your word is a lamp for my feet,
a light on my path.

1 Peter 2:9

But you are a chosen people, a royal priesthood, a holy nation, God's special possession, that you may declare the praises of him who called you out of darkness into his wonderful light. 10 Once you were not a people, but now you are the people of God; once you had not received mercy, but now you have received mercy.

THESE ARE THE TIMES

"Run to Me when you make poor choices, in prayer and repentance, and to fortify yourself with My promises in Scripture. These are the times to sit and meditate on My perfection and listen for My still, small voice. These are the times to expand your trust and grow your faith by focusing on Me. These are the times to fall to your knees in thankfulness and gratitude, praising and worshiping your Savior for the new life I have given you.

"Choose not to dwell on that which is not of Me—for the enemy's desire is for the shame to engulf you, for the retribution to torment you, and for the poor choices to define you. But My words and promises are the opposite to that of the enemy.

"You are loved unconditionally. I have forgiven you so totally that I remember your sin no more. I promise to protect you always, and because you belong to Me, we will live together in Eternity. My merciful love includes discipline and correction, but this comes from the place of My perfect love. I want nothing but the best for you—and the enemy hates this. He does not want God's good and vast Plan for your life to unfold, and he most certainly does not want God to be glorified by your life.

"Living in the fallen world, and with your sinful nature still living inside of you, you will make choices that are not of Me. Yet if you keep your eyes fixed on your merciful and loving Savior, I will bring us through. If you stay close to Me and My promises, you emerge victorious in Me. Remember My love, My forgiveness, and My goodness and grace, and we cannot lose. You are overcomers in Me."

MEREDITH SWIFT

Psalm 103:1
Praise the LORD, my soul;
all my inmost being, praise his holy name.
2 Praise the Lord, my soul,
and forget not all his benefits—
3 who forgives all your sins
and heals all your diseases,
4 who redeems your life from the pit
and crowns you with love and compassion,
5 who satisfies your desires with good things
so that your youth is renewed like the eagle's.

Hebrews 8:10
This is the covenant I will establish with the people of Israel
after that time, declares the Lord. I will put my laws in their minds and
write them on their hearts. I will be their God, and they will be my people.

SEEDS FROM YOUR HEART

"Your children, those seeds from your heart, belong to Me before they belong to you. As much as you love them, I love them more. They are given into your care to provide for them, build character in them, nurture them, discipline them, grow them up and love them—not with a love that is suffocating, but with a love that sets them up for independence and for being equipped to walk their life's path.

"Follow My precepts found in My Holy Scriptures for the way to bring your children to adulthood. Give them a love grounded in Me, knowing that when they are grown I am still there to catch them when they fall. For you are always My children, My precious children of God, and I am always and eternally your loving Father.

"Pray for your children! Ask Me for the guidance and assistance you need. For the enemy will use the ones closest in your heart to target. Fall on your knees as you let your tears flow and lay bare what is within your heart. Bring all your pain and uncertainty and fear around how best to care for your children to Me. When it is brought out into the open it can be addressed.

"Yet sometimes the wordless groaning of your heart is the way to pray to Me, when the pain of a situation is too difficult and raw to express in words. Where your children are concerned this is often what will happen.

"Your children have their own path to follow, their own destiny, their own journey. My Plan for them is good. So do not allow fear to overtake this truth. For all who believe will return to Me; all who believe in Me belong to Me; and I am faithful; My promises are sound."

MEREDITH SWIFT

Psalm 127:3
Children are a heritage from the LORD, offspring a reward from him.

Ezekiel 18:4
For everyone belongs to me, the parent as well as the child—both alike belong to me.

PROTECTOR, CONQUERER, OVERCOMER, ENDURER

"I am the same yesterday, today, and tomorrow. I am the constant in a world of instability, the calm in the storm, the order amongst the chaos, the rock upon which all can place their faith. I am the Protector, the Conqueror, the Overcomer, the Endurer, the King of Kings, Lord of Lords, Prince of Peace. I am the Lord Jesus Christ. I am the rock that you anchor yourselves to, the faith and forgiveness that sets you free.

"You could be in the heights of exhilaration or in the depths of despair, you could be facing the most intolerable injustice and persecution or you could be riding high in a season of happiness where everything is going your way. The message of your King of Kings is that I am Lord in every situation. Circumstances are transient but I am constant and faithful.

"Joy in all circumstances. Your eyes only on Me. Praising Me and giving thanks to Me for every part of your lives that you find yourselves in, for surely I am guiding your footsteps and most assuredly My plan for you is *good*. All things are working together for the good of those who love Me.

"Because of My love for you, My deep and true and abiding and sacrificial love, unconditional and eternal, because of My delight in you, because of My covenant of oneness with My creation—I work all things together for your good. So you can rest in Me, safely, knowing that in all circumstances I am there—your Rock, your Shepherd, your Protector, your Saviour.

"I am Lord. Praise Me!"

2 Samuel 22:3
My God is my rock, in whom I take refuge, my shield and the horn of my
salvation. He is my stronghold, my refuge and my savior—from violent
people you save me.

Proverbs 8:30
Then I was constantly at his side.
I was filled with delight day after day,
rejoicing always in his presence,
31 rejoicing in his whole world
and delighting in mankind.
32 "Now then, my children, listen to me;
blessed are those who keep my ways.
33 Listen to my instruction and be wise;
do not disregard it.

ESSENTIAL MOVEMENT

"Your faith is a walk. So movement is essential. Faith without works is dead. So action is vital. Anything that keeps you journeying with Me. Physical movement. Emotional movement. Mental movement. Demonstrating My love for your brothers and sisters by your actions, your thoughts, and your prayers. There are times of waiting on My will to be revealed, but inaction does not have to mean there is no movement. Prayer is movement. It is the action of communication with Me.

"I work in movement—through people, places, things, thoughts, and events. I am the Creator of all that is, so I am able to use all that is for My glorification. So prayer is essential to recognizing what it is I would wish for you. Listening for My voice. Being prompted by the Holy Spirit's guidance. When you are open to the Lord of the Universe you will begin to see My handiwork everywhere. You begin to see the inherent joy in all of creation. As you walk with Me in thankfulness and gratitude, you begin to realize the gift of life and the gift of My grace drenched forgiveness upon your life.

"For I adore you, you who are the apple of My eye, and I gave up all I had for you and to forge a new covenant relationship with you. What was given up then now continues on with My goodness and grace and mercy and the promise of Eternity with Me.

"The enemy is the opposite—he seeks to paralyze you through fear and doubt, keeping you enslaved to *re*action, seeking you to be shriveled and lost within his tormenting thoughts. Yet I, the Lord of the Universe, find you, pick you up and carry you, take your burdens, give you My strength, and propel you forward into My love and Holy grace.

"So walk forward with Me, precious child. And allow this journey of faith to begin to gain momentum until you are running into My arms, running with joy at the knowledge that you were created by the Lord of the Universe, the King of Kings, for just such a time as this. And let this race you are running towards Me bring you security and rest and peace and joy.

"Run headlong into the Plan I have for your life, embrace it fully as you embrace your Creator God, with every fiber of your being. For I am within, without, above, below, in front of and behind you in every single moment of our journey in faith. For I love you!"

> *Habakkuk 3:18*
> *Yet I will rejoice in the Lord, I will be joyful in God my Savior. 19 The Sovereign LORD is my strength; he makes my feet like the feet of a deer, he enables me to tread on the heights.*

REFLECTION:
ONE LOST LITTLE SHEEP

Feeding the 5,000 was a miracle to the disciples of Jesus. To Jesus, though, it was a straightforward case of seeing a need and filling it. People were hungry; He made sure they were fed. He sees the need in us for Him and when we come to Him, He makes sure we are nourished by the unending love He has for us.

This is the foundational principle of the teachings of Jesus—love for our Lord God Almighty and love for one another as an outflow of His love for us. His perfect love for us gave Him the willingness to take on our sin and die for us. We should do the same—that is, we die to our old sinful lifestyle and are willing to live in the way our Lord Jesus Christ has decreed. This is the price we, as chosen and cherished children of God, must willingly pay. We have been purchased at the Cross with the blood of our Savior; His sacrifice has paid our debt in full. We are no longer under the weight of sin. We are forgiven and freed in the mightiness of His glorious grace.

When I am with Lord Jesus in the Garden of Promise I know that He is Sovereign, He is my King and my Lord. I am reverent towards Him; I bow down before Him. Yet He is also my Savior and Creator and the one who loves me with a love I cannot fathom, with a limitless depth and breadth. He is so comforting and strong. So the awe I have for Him is one part of my relationship with Him; the other part is the acceptance and the absolute love that flows from Him. I am one little sheep from His flock, yet He as my Shepherd cares and ministers to me in a way that brings such security. I am valued and important to Him. He comes in search of me to bring me back to His flock.

Jesus came in search of me and He found me. He brought me back to His flock. He brought my heart back to Him so that He could take care of it. He takes care of my heart so beautifully and tenderly because He is so completely trustworthy. Trust is given to those who keep their promises. Lord Jesus has never broken a promise to any of His children. He *cannot* break a promise. That is not part of His character. He is completely trustworthy.

In so many ways, His ways are unfathomable and mysterious. Yet in other ways they are so transparent, for He is so loving, faithful, merciful, and constant. He demonstrates this over and over again in Scripture. And through the provision of His Holy Spirit, He demonstrates this in the personal relationship each believer can have with Him. How could I ever have resisted His call upon my life?

Yet I did resist, for quite a long time. I felt scared and fearful and made excuses not to heed His call. Eventually, His love for me won out. Yet I still had to make the choice. I could never have imagined how making the choice for Jesus Christ was the first step on a journey towards a transformation that has been and is, to say the least, radical. Transformation from the inside out, occurring on so many levels of my life and in so many ways that it is impossible to adequately express its profoundness.

This silly, scared, forlorn, and lost little sheep, bleating with fear, was finally able to recognize that not only did I have a Shepherd who had always protected me, but also a Savior who had given me true freedom. A miracle-working, fierce protector who gave me freedom at the Cross, crushing sin and death with the power of His blood. At the Cross, the enemy of the world lost his power over death and the Lord of all Creation purchased eternal inheritance for those who accept Him. The prowling enemy, like a roaring lion looking for someone to devour, was no match for Jesus, the mighty Lion of Judah.

And so, in this Garden of Promise with my Lord Jesus, I am profoundly grateful for the gift of salvation He offered to me. Profoundly thankful that I accepted this gift. Profoundly humbled by His perfect love that paid my debt of sin in full. Paid in full by His precious and Holy blood poured out for me. For *me*. Hallelujah! All praise and glory to You Lord!

Thank You, Lord Jesus, thank You!

> *Psalm 33:18*
> *But the eyes of the LORD are on those who fear him, on those whose hope is in his unfailing love.*

> *John 10:16*
> *I have other sheep that are not of this sheep pen. I must bring them also. They too will listen to My voice, and there shall be one flock and one shepherd.*

CONCLUSION

FOR YOU HAVE
BEEN GIVEN THIS LIFE

The brick wall has disappeared completely now and light floods the Garden.

"And so, My precious and cherished child, we come to the end of our communication for now. You who were hidden away in shame, in fear, without trust, without safety and security, are now lifted up into My loving arms, My perpetual embrace, and My eternal sovereignty. Remember, My lost little sheep, that you are now found and never again will you be alone, never again will you be without the protection of the One who set you free, of the One who called your name to come, the One who was with you before the beginning of time, the One who loves you without condition and with a vastness of purity that is limitless.

"Walk with Me, your Creator God. Live in faith and allow that faith to expand you and transform you. Allow that faith to keep you in step and in check as you live within the Plan I have for your good and My glory. For you have been given this life, this glorious, grace-filled life—to LIVE!!! To truly live within My body, within My promises, guided by My Holy Scriptures and My Holy Spirit, to live with the truth that we are together now and for all of Eternity.

"Be blessed as you rest within Me. Safe and secure, protected, forgiven, sanctified, and justified . . . and truly, truly, truly loved. For I am close by, always. Close by, always. Peace be with you."

Habakkuk 2:2
Then the LORD replied:
"Write down the revelation and make it plain on tablets
so that a herald may run with it.
3 For the revelation awaits an appointed time;
it speaks of the end
and will not prove false.
Though it linger, wait for it;
it will certainly come
and will not delay.
4 "See, the enemy is puffed up;
his desires are not upright—
but the righteous person will live by his faithfulness.

Romans 10:9
If you declare with your mouth, "Jesus is Lord," and believe in your heart
that God raised him from the dead, you will be saved. 10 For it is with
your heart that you believe and are justified, and it is with your mouth that
you profess your faith and are saved.

As the previous Scripture shows, we can be saved if we call on Lord Jesus to come into our hearts, renouncing our past lives of sin, and seeking a new life with Him. We are created to be in relationship with God and to be saved through faith in Jesus Christ. I pray that if you do not know Jesus already that you now want to know Him and forge a close relationship with Him.

Accepting Jesus and the beginning of having a close relationship with Him is a simple matter of praying this prayer:

"Dear Lord Jesus. I ask you into my heart today, to live within me, to guide me and love me. I know I have lived a life of sin and I am sorry for this and I turn from that life now. I acknowledge that you took my sin when you died on the Cross for me and I accept your gift of forgiveness and salvation. I want to follow you all the days of my life now. I pray this prayer in faith in the name of Jesus. Amen."

Welcome to the family of God! God bless you!

Now, your next step is to connect with a bible believing Church. Please contact me at www.meredithswiftauthor.com if you need assistance with this.

ACKNOWLEDGEMENTS
AND THANKS

First and foremost, I acknowledge and thank my Lord Jesus Christ for saving me and setting me free. I thank and praise Him for writing this book through me and for His guidance and provision over all aspects of this book. To God be the glory!

A huge and heartfelt acknowledgement and thank you to the following people for their part in bringing this book to fruition. I have been truly blessed by these amazing people:

My beautiful and precious daughters Sarah and Melissa for being who you are. I love you both more than words can say.

My wonderful sister Debby, who has been a rock solid and safe harbor all my life. I love you so very much.

Steve and Linda Ballin for your support and grace during some very turbulent times of my life. You two showed me the love of Jesus and your Church, SugarReef Baptist Church, Ingham, Queensland, Australia will always hold a very special place in my heart.

All the wonderful friends at SugarReef Baptist Church, Ingham, for being my first Church family (2010-2015).

All the wonderful friends at Calvary Christian Church, Townsville, for being my second Church family (2016-2017).

Rosetta, Jean (who led me to Christ), and Sandra, my very special Sisters-in-Christ, for your love and support. My life is all the richer because you are in it.

Kathy Anderson, Niesje Delano (Founder of J.E.M. Studios), Carole Desf, Mimi Emmanuel, Kimberly Hausbeck, Paul Hughes, Sunny Kang, Susan Kay, Anna Mogan, Molly, Tina Pocernich, Mie Potter, Jason and Summer Sterner, Carolyn Thomson Twaddle, Virginia, JWang, Jackie Weisser and the rest of my incredibly supportive Launch Team; Peta Soorkia and Angela Curtis for helping bring this book out into the world. I could not have done this without you.

To YOU for reading my book! I pray you have found it a blessing and an encouragement. I would welcome your feedback and questions. Connect with me at www.meredithswiftauthor.com. It would be much appreciated if you could leave a helpful review on Amazon to let me know what you thought of my book. You can go to Amazon.com and type in Hearing His Voice—Meeting Jesus in the Garden of Promise. Once you are there, scroll down to the reviews section and share your thoughts in the "Write a Customer Review" box. Thank you so much!

Chandler Bolt, Sean Sumner and all the team at Self-Publishing School for providing the blueprint for writing and publishing this book.

SELF-PUBLISHING
SCHOOL

NOW IT'S YOUR TURN

**Discover the EXACT 3-step blueprint you need to
become a bestselling author in 3 months.**

Self-Publishing School helped me, and now I want
them to help you with this FREE WEBINAR!

Even if you're busy, bad at writing, or don't know where to start, you
CAN write a bestseller and build your best life.

With tools and experience across a variety niches and professions, Self-
Publishing School is the only resource
you need to take your book to the finish line!

DON'T WAIT

Watch this FREE WEBINAR now,
and Say "YES" to becoming a bestseller:

[https://xe172.isrefer.com/go/curcust/bookbrosinc1809]

ABOUT THE AUTHOR

Meredith Swift grew up in rural Victoria, on a dairy farm, the second youngest of five children.

She has lived in quite a few different places and now calls sunny Townsville, in Far North Queensland, her home.

Meredith has two daughters, two cats and a golden retriever.

As well as being involved in the life of her church, Meredith enjoys travel, bushwalking, cooking and reading.

CPSIA information can be obtained
at www.ICGtesting.com
Printed in the USA
LVHW081252300619
622771LV00038B/1299/P

9 780648 507314